THE
E-BOAT
THREAT

THE E-BOAT THREAT

BRYAN COOPER

A MACDONALD ILLUSTRATED WAR STUDY

Macdonald and Jane's · London

OTHER BOOKS BY BRYAN COOPER

Non-fiction

North Sea Oil – The Great Gamble
The Ironclads of Cambrai
The Battle of the Torpedo Boats
The Buccaneers
Alaska – The Last Frontier
Fighter
Tank Battles of World War 1
Bomber
The Adventure of North Sea Oil

Novels

Stones of Evil
The Wildcatters

All the photographs are from The Imperial War Museum, with the following exceptions: the photograph on the title page and page 6 are from Brian L. Davis, that on page 62 is from Drüppel and those on pages 78 and 80 are from Beken of Cowes.

First published in 1976 by
Macdonald and Jane's Publishers Limited
Paulton House, 8 Shepherdess Walk
London N1 7LW

Printed in Great Britain by
REDWOOD BURN LIMITED
Trowbridge & Esher

ISBN 0 356 08144 3

Drawings and Diagrams by Peter Endsleigh Castle AMRAeS

CONTENTS

Introduction   7

Early Development   13

World War II Line-Up   21

Merchant Shipping Under Attack   29

E-boats in Action   39

Growing Threat to Coastal Convoys   49

Coastal Forces Strike Back   57

New Boats   71

In the Balance   81

Coastal Forces Take the Offensive   93

Stalemate   105

Fight to the End   113

Epilogue   127

Appendix 1 Anti-E-boat Weapons   130

Appendix 2 Mines   132

Bibliography   134

Index   135

INTRODUCTION

All the major powers that fought in World War II, with the exception of Japan, built large numbers of motor torpedo boats specifically to operate in coastal waters. These highly manoeuvrable 'little ships', when they met in action, were involved in some of the closest-fought sea battles of the war. But their main function was to attack much larger enemy vessels, either merchant shipping or warships, by using the striking power of their torpedoes.

The main advantages of motor torpedo boats were their size and speed. They were small enough to move largely unseen at night, with sufficiently shallow draught to pass safely over enemy minefields. They were fast enough, with speeds of 40 knots and more, either to roar up on enemy ships to attack them broadside or, what was often preferable, to make a rapid escape after creeping up slowly and quietly on the enemy. Once their torpedoes had been fired, the little ships needed speed to get away before the enemy's guns could be brought to bear on them. One further advantage was that such craft could be built relatively cheaply in numerous boatyards, leaving the more specialised shipyards free to concentrate on building warships.

But motor torpedo boats had their disadvantages as well. Because weight of armament had to be sacrificed to speed, they were especially vulnerable to attack by enemy aircraft and this usually limited their operations to the hours of darkness. Because of the high fuel-consumption of their powerful engines, range was limited to a few hundred miles unless auxiliary gasoline tanks were carried. And because of their size and light construction – necessary factors in achieving high speeds – motor torpedo boats could not operate in very heavy seas. Even in less rough conditions they were prone to mechanical breakdown. Nevertheless, it was extraordinary what a hammering they could take and still survive. The men who crewed these night hunters might curse the buffeting they

Opposite: *Camouflaged E-boat returning to base after an operational sortie*

got, but as they rode the waves with bows lifted and wakes foaming a long trail behind, they knew an exhilaration of speed that no other kind of ship could give.

In spite of the very considerable damage they caused, the motor torpedo boats of all the major navies were too small and numerous to be given the dignity of individual names and were known by numbers instead. To the British they were MTBs (Motor Torpedo Boat), to the Americans PT-boats (Patrol Torpedo), to the Italians MAS-boats (Motoscafo Anti-Sommergibile), and to the Germans S-boats (Schnellboot, meaning fast boat). For some curious and unexplained reason, the Schnellboot was always referred to by the British Navy as an E-boat, presumably standing for 'Enemy' war motorboat. This term could, of course, be applied to many other enemy craft and would have caused only confusion rather than aiding identification. In fact, in all other instances, the British Navy used the initial letter of the actual German word for describing a particular type of craft. Had this been done in the case of motor torpedo boats, they would have been known rightly as S-boats, as they were to the Germans. Several suggestions have been put forward to explain this, including the ingenious theory that the 'E' might have stood for the technical term 'Lürssen Effekt' (one of the features introduced into their boats in the 1930s by the Lürssen shipyard which later became responsible for building most of the German S-boats). It is probable, however, that the real explanation is the simplest and that the 'E' was meant to stand merely for Enemy. Both before and at the beginning of the war, these craft (whether British or German) were not taken very seriously by the Admiralty, and it is likely that the definition was rather thoughtlessly coined in the belief that it would seldom be used. Although the Germans also developed motor boats for other purposes, such as the Lürssen R-boats (Räumboot) which were used for minelaying, minesweeping and coastal convoy protection when it was armed with 37mm and 20mm guns, these were referred to by their correct prefixes, so that the Royal Navy's E-boat designation stood only for motor torpedo boats.

Whatever they were called, motor torpedo boats fought very successfully in the coastal waters of every major theatre of the war – in the North Sea and English Channel, the Mediterranean and among the dreamy islands of the Aegean, the Baltic, off Burma and Malaya and in the South China Sea, and across the Pacific to the final liberation of the Philippines. Probably their most wide-scale use was in the Pacific, largely by the United States for the Japanese did less than any other naval power to develop such craft, mainly due to chronic lack of suitable engines. Thus there was nothing comparable to combat the American PT-boats as they took part in the island-hopping strategy to liberate Japanese-occupied territories. PT-boats were used to attack coastal supply ships, they cooperated closely with the US Army during troop landings, and took part in some of the great fleet battles in the Pacific where they were effective in sinking Japanese warships up to the size of light cruiser. The Mediterranean conflict saw the biggest variety of craft. The British, Americans, Germans and Italians used motor torpedo boats both to attack as well as to defend convoys as both sides fought desperately to keep open lines of supply to their land forces. Malta and Sicily featured prominently in this struggle, as bases respectively for British and Axis craft. The large canvas of Mediterranean operations gave considerable scope for the kind of lone role that suited the individualistic temperament of those who served in the little ships. As well as their main purpose of attacking enemy convoys, MTBs and PT-boats took part in commando raids and co-operated with partisans fighting behind enemy lines. Large numbers of Italian MAS-boats played a part in the early stages of the war, since Italy had given more attention than the other powers to the military application of such craft and had the largest number of them. At one point in the war, an American PT-squadron was the only representative of the US Navy in the Mediterranean.

However, the fiercest motor torpedo boat battles were fought in the seas off the east and south coasts of Britain, and it is with these operations that this book is concerned. With Germany's occupation of France and the whole coastline of Western Europe, the E-boats had bases from which to launch a concerted attack on Britain's vital east coast shipping. Further targets were of course available in the overseas convoys bringing goods and supplies into Britain, but as these were usually well escorted when close to British ports, it was against the more vulnerable coastal convoys that the E-boats directed their main attack. This included direct attack by torpedo and the more indirect attack of laying mines on the convoy routes, overall the more successful of the two. At the same time, British MTBs were similarly used to attack German coastal shipping. But there was a marked difference in the make-up of the two navies, in that the Germans had less coastal shipping and more armed escorts to protect it, whereas the British at any one time had several hundred merchant ships sailing up or down the east coast and few escort vessels available to protect them. Such was the havoc caused by the E-boats in their nightly raids along E-boat Alley – the main convoy route off the coast of East Anglia – that special motor gunboats (MGBs) were designed to combat them. It was in the North Sea that battles raged between the British and German craft, fought hand to hand at closer quarters than any other kind of warship. The Germans held the upper hand until the end of 1942, when Britain's Coastal Forces (as the MTB and MGB flotillas were known) began to reach equal terms with the E-boat, in many ways the best of all motor torpedo boats used during the war. The fighting increased in intensity in 1943 and again in 1944 with the Normandy landings. It was at this time that American PT-boats first appeared in British waters, helping the MTBs to protect the Allied supply routes from harrassment by the German boats. Although by then outnumbered and out-classed, the

E-boat crews fought tenaciously until the very end of the war, when they were still doing their best to sink Allied shipping.

Motor torpedo boat warfare was, however, built up from very small beginnings. Although such craft had been used very successfully during World War I, especially by the Italians against the Austrians, they were largely neglected by Britain and the USA in the inter-war period. Even in Germany, they were originally developed mainly as a means of getting around the terms of the Versailles Treaty. It was the attitude of most nations with large navies that the bigger the ship, the better. Little was done officially to develop motor torpedo boats, and most of the essential research carried out was by private companies and individuals, largely for sport and pleasure. Record-breaking attempts by men such as Sir Malcolm Campbell and Sir Henry Segrave provided much valuable knowledge on fast boat design, and the German Schnellboot was, in fact, based on the design for a motor launch built privately for an American customer by the Lürssen yard. At the same time, smaller nations – perhaps because they could not so easily build big ships – were very much alive to the possibilities of motor torpedo boats. Companies like Vosper and Thornycroft built MTBs for many foreign navies, some of them later to be used against the Allies. Because of the interchange of ideas and equipment between countries which were later to find themselves on opposing sides, there was an extraordinary situation at the beginning of the war in which the few British MTBs that were in service were powered by Italian Isotta-Fraschini engines, the best small-boat petrol engine designed at that time but one which naturally became unavailable when Italy entered the war. Such was the even greater neglect in the USA that an MTB design by the British Power Boat Company was used as the basis for most of the American PT-boats. The American Packard engine which became the main power unit for all British and American boats was itself a development of the Rolls-Royce Merlin engine. Japan did least of all to develop fast fighting boats, and the very few that were built were based on a Thornycroft design.

One of the lessons that had to be re-learnt in World War II – for the same has been true of nearly every war in this century – is the vital importance of coastal waters. Not only must merchant ships from abroad bring in supplies through such waters, but often, coastal convoys are the only practical and economic means of taking materials from one part of a country to another. These convoys must be protected, while at the same time, plans must be made to attack those of the enemy. From a purely military point of view, coastal waters must be a major factor to be taken into account in mounting any expeditionary raid or invasion. This involves both offensive and defensive considerations. The evacuation from Dunkirk was possibly only because Britain held a balance of power in the English Channel. Germany's plan to invade Britain failed because this vital command of that narrow sea was lacking.

Small fighting craft are, of course, only one weapon involved in any consideration of coastal waters. Other ships have a part to play, such as destroyers which were feared more by the German E-boat commanders than the motor gunboats specifically designed to be used against them. But a combination of the two, destroyers and MGBs, was even more effective, as later operations in the North Sea proved. Air power played a major role, especially by day and even more particularly in the laying of mines than in direct attack against enemy shipping. Again, it was most successful when used in cooperation with other forces, and by mid-1943, for instance, MTBs had found it extremely useful to work with Fighter Command in offensive sweeps against German shipping between the Dutch coast and the Channel approaches. With fighter cover overhead to ward off any attacks by enemy aircraft, MTBs could go further afield and risk returning during the daylight hours after a night's operations. In return, those same craft might have sunk a flak ship in the North Sea and thereby saved, perhaps, an RAF torpedo-bomber during an attack the next day on a German convoy. A growing appreciation of the inter-dependence between the different Services was an important feature of the war.

EARLY DEVELOPMENT

Up until the latter part of the the 18th Century, it was generally thought that the force of an underwater explosion would be dissipated by the water and could not harm the hull of a ship, even when detonated close to it. There were a few exceptions. One of Queen Elizabeth I's admirals, Sir William Monson, realised that a vessel is more vulnerable below the water-line than above it, although there is no record that he ever carried out his plan to fire a cannon from the hold of a barque laid alongside an enemy ship. At the siege of Antwerp in 1585, the Dutch destroyed 800 Spaniards by a contrivance they called an explosion vessel, fitted with clockwork mechanism. Seventy years later the Marquis of Worcester invented a ship-destroying engine which, like the Dutch device, was actuated by clockwork but also required a diver to attach it to the ship which was to be attacked. This invention does not appear to have been used. As with all the early inventors of mines, the problem they failed to overcome.was the elimination of the human agency to operate the device.

It was left to an American engineer, David Bushnell – also known as the father of the submarine – to evolve the idea of detonating mines by contact. In 1775 he invented what he called a torpedo but which was in fact a floating mine. The true torpedo, which could be regarded as a development of the mine, but one propelled through the water under its own power, did not come until a hundred years later. Bushnell demonstrated his idea against British shipping during the American War of Independence, when several vessels were sunk, but he was unable to arouse much official interest and eventually, an embittered man, he gave up. Twenty years later another American, Robert Fulton, resurrected the idea. Better known as the designer and builder of the first practical steamship, he invented a mine and also a crude submarine, which he called a 'plunging-boat', from which to fire it. Britain and France were at war at the time and in circumstances of great cloak-and-dagger intrigue

Fulton tried to interest first the French and then the British in his inventions. But in spite of dramatic and highly successful demonstrations, as when Fulton blew up a large ship in the Thames before an invited audience of naval and military leaders, capturing the interest of both Napoleon and Mr. Pitt, the two navies refused to support the development of such weapons. It was not only a reaction against something new that contradicted all previously held theories, as Bushnell had found, or a feeling that the new invention was barbaric and unfitted to chivalrous war, an attitude expressed particularly by French naval officers. Both sides, as maritime powers, instinctively realised the threat that such inventions posed to large fleets on which their power was based. They were not going to help with the development of weapons that would put them at the mercy of any country, however small, which only had to manufacture and lay a few mines in the right places.

This attitude was later reflected in the lukewarm approach of the major naval powers to the development of motor torpedo boats. Again, they posed a threat to the big fleets, clearly seen by Admiral von Tirpitz when in the 1880s, soon after the invention of the modern torpedo, he wrote: 'small navies are now gaining in importance when strong armour is no longer sufficient to blockade them in their ports. Through the torpedo, the general suitability of small navies for making war will be revived as a serious factor.'

To return to Fulton, however, he retired discomfited to the United States where again he proved the possibilities of submarine mines. But they were not used effectively until war broke out between Germany and Denmark in 1848 when Professor Himmly, unaware of either Bushnell's or Fulton's work, invented a mine which could be detonated by electric contact from the shore. The first mines to be laid as weapons of defence were used to protect Kiel against the Danish fleet. The Russians also laid mines to defend the ports of Sevastopol and Kronstadt during the Crimean War.

The first extensive use of mines (still called torpedoes at the time) came during the American Civil War when the Confederates tried to equalise their inferiority in ships by minelaying. Although not a single vessel on either side was sunk by gunfire, nearly thirty were destroyed by contact mines. Some were made of beer-kegs with chemical fuses; others were truncated tin cones with gunpowder in the lower end and on the top an iron cap which was displaced on contact and pulled a friction tube, thus detonating the charge. Captain Hunter Davidson, a Confederate officer, went one step further when in 1864 he developed the idea of tying an explosive charge on the end of a pole mounted over the bows of a rowing boat and setting off at night to ram enemy ships. Considerable damage was caused in this way, although the attackers were often blown up together with those attacked (Davidson himself survived). However, in its primitive way, his concept was a forerunner of the torpedo boat.

Other nations and individuals took it up when the war was over. One was an Austrian frigate captain, Giovanni Luppis, who experimented with a self-propelled boat, driven by a clockwork motor, which carried an explosive charge in its bows. The boat was steered and the charge released by means of remote cable controls. Luppis tried to interest an English engineer, Robert Whitehead, in the idea. Whitehead at that time was manager of a firm of engine builders at Fiume in Yugoslavia. He built a model based on the Austrian's concept, but then rejected it as impractical. Instead, he turned his own attention to the possibility of making an explosive charge that could travel through water under its own power. In 1877 he completed his first self-propelled torpedo, powered by a compressed-air engine driving a single propeller that gave a speed of 6 knots and a range of 700 yards. During that same year, the mine, which up until then had been regarded solely as a defensive weapon, was used offensively for the first time; in the Russo-Turkish War a small party of Russians swam across the lower Danube towing an electro-controlled mine which they placed under the bottom of a Turkish warship. When the mine was fired, the ship was blown to pieces and not a man on board saved. Thus were developed the two weapons – the mine and the torpedo – which were to revolutionise warfare at sea.

Meanwhile, shipbuilders in Britain and Germany had already been building steam-powered torpedo-boats fitted with the same kind of 'spar torpedo' projecting over the bows that Davidson had developed. One of the first was built by Yarrow in 1872, using a 30-foot steam-driven launch, and such craft were already in world-wide demand when Whitehead's self-propelled torpedo became available. It was simply a matter of exchanging the fixed spar torpedo for a torpedo tube, and the torpedo boat in a modern sense had arrived. Navies throughout the world were soon clamouring for the new weapon, seeing in it a means of combating the biggest ships afloat, just as the British and French naval leaders had foreseen back in Bushnell's time. When firms like Yarrow could not keep up with the demand, builders in other countries were soon busy designing craft of their own. The great advantage was that nothing very complicated was required in the way of guns or armour-plate, as in the case of larger warships. In place of these, the new torpedo boats relied on higher speed and the striking power of their torpedoes.

Alarmed at these developments the major naval powers, particularly Britain and Germany, looked for ways of countering the torpedo boats that threatened their big but relatively slow ships. In 1892, Alfred Yarrow suggested to the Admiralty the need for a fast, more heavily armed ship that could chase and destroy such craft. With the approval of the Royal Navy he put the same machinery as in a 500-ton gunboat into a 250-ton vessel designed to attack torpedo boats. This ship, the *Hornet*, was the first of a new class that became known throughout the world as the destroyer. The original function of destroyers was to fight torpedo boats. But from

E·BOAT

KEY TO E-BOAT STUDY

1	20mm AA gun mounted in foredeck well	8	Starboard
2	20mm AA gun limit-rail protecting bridge	9	Spare torpedo on deck chocks port & starboard
3	Hinged cover to enclosed bow torpedo-tubes	10	Stowage for two rubber dinghies
4	Pre-cast armoured cupola bridge ('Kallotte')	11	Stowage for single rubber dinghy
5	Bridge ports with folding armour shields	12	After deck armament (Twin 20mm AA gun or
6	Aerial lead-in		37mm AA gun (shown) or 40mm Bofors fitted
7	Radio & Radar antennae		to late series E-Boats)

13   *Stern launching gear for mines (Contact, Acoustic, Pressure or Magnetic types)*
14   *Triple propellers (Centre propeller used for slow running) with one main & two side aerofoil-shaped rudders*
15   *Deck rails usually covered with canvas side screens (omitted to show detail)*

the start, they were themselves armed with torpedoes so that they operated as torpedo boats as well. In the race to achieve naval supremacy during the years leading up to World War I, both the torpedo boats on which the Germans concentrated and the destroyers built by Britain and America became rapidly bigger as heavier guns were fitted and then larger engines had to be installed to maintain the same speed. What started in concept as a torpedo-carrying boat had become a vessel of 1,000 tons and more. And its very size created new problems, not only because it was now a larger and easier target but because of its vulnerability to mines. There was still a need, although it was only vaguely seen at the time, for a small torpedo boat of the kind originally intended.

The first boats had, of course, been driven by steam engines which took up a lot of space and whose power-to-weight ratio restricted maximum speeds. This situation was abruptly changed with the invention of the internal combustion engine and the possibilities that were opened up of driving boats by means of small petrol or diesel engines. One of the first in the field was Otto Lürssen, owner of a yacht- and boat-yard at Bremen-Vegesack. He built his first motor boat in 1890, and by 1908 was able to achieve 18 knots with his 40 hp launch *Donnerwetter*. By this time boatbuilders in other countries had joined in the pursuit of providing fast motor boats for sport and pleasure, notably the SVAN company in Italy and John I. Thornycroft in Britain. International competition was fierce, and a 'Championship of the Seas' race at Monaco in 1911 was won by Lürssen's latest boat, the *Lürssen-Daimler*, powered by two 102 hp engines. Strangely, however, after the earlier interest that had been shown in torpedo boats, the possibility of using motor-driven craft for this purpose was neglected by most of the major powers. The USA entered the field in 1908 when ten motor torpedo boats based on a Lewis Nixon design were built for Russia. But although plans for 115-foot and 150-foot craft were drawn up, intended for coastal defence, the US Navy saw little use for small boats and they were not built.

In Britain also, the Royal Navy showed little interest in the motor torpedo boats being designed and built by Thornycroft for other navies, and had ordered none before World War I broke out. The same applied in Germany, with the exception that a passing interest was shown in a remote-controlled boat packed with explosives that was built as an experiment by Wilhelm von Siemens. He invested a considerable amount of money in the project, and the *Havel I* which he built in 1911 was able to run at 30 knots, controlled by two long wires which could take the boat up to an enemy warship and then explode it. The Imperial Navy carried out some trials, then dropped the idea. As in Britain and America, destroyers were seen as the most practical surface vessels for carrying torpedoes, and efforts were concentrated on building larger types of these.

It came as a shock to the British Navy after World War I started to see the extent to which Germany intended to use mines and torpedo-carrying submarines, and to find out how vulnerable their big ships were to these weapons, although they were hardly new, as their early history has shown. The Grand Fleet itself was lucky to escape becoming entangled with the first minefield to be laid, in the Southwold area, by steaming northwards only a few days before. With the big ships bottled up and hardly daring to leave port, the Admiralty had to think in terms of smaller craft to combat the German submarines, torpedo boats and minelayers, and also to sweep the convoy routes clear of mines. A wide range of vessels were built or pressed into service for these purposes, including trawlers, whalers, patrol gunboats, yachts, and paddle or screw mine-sweepers, manned almost entirely by volunteers including the Royal Naval Volunteer Reserve. Among these was a type of boat known as the Coastal Motor Boat (CMB), forerunner of the World War II MTBs. It was suggested by three young Royal Naval lieutenants who saw the possibility of using motor boats to go safely over the minefields off the German coast in order to attack enemy bases. Built by Thornycroft, the CMBs were torpedo-carrying boats capable of 33.5 knots, originally 40 feet in length but later increased to 55 feet. They first came into service in 1916 and 66 were in commission by the end of the war. They were responsible for some dramatic and successful actions off the Belgian coast in the latter stages of the war, particularly the Zeebrugge and Ostend raids. But their most spectacular success was just after the war, when in 1919 during a raid on Kronstadt (following the revolution in Russia) they sank a cruiser and disabled two capital ships and two destroyers for the loss of only one CMB.

The Germans had less need for such craft, but in 1916 it was decided that Lürssen's fast motor boat might be refitted as a despatch boat. Acting on his own authority, Lürssen fitted a torpedo-tube over the bows of his racy vessel. This apparently impressed the naval authorities, for they immediately ordered a second boat of the same type complete with torpedo tube (which was, however, removed from the first boat whose duties were restricted to carrying despatches). The second boat was delivered in April 1917 and given the title of *Sonderkommando Gleitboot*, powered by two 240 hp engines which gave a speed of 30 knots. In September of that year it was successful in sinking a 5,000-ton cargo ship. This action moved the Naval Staff to order a number of fast motor torpedo boats late in 1917 for use against British warships off the Belgian coast. The few craft that had been completed by the end of the war were each powered by three aero engines which gave a maximum of 32 knots, but they were not a success as the petrol engines failed or caught fire. All development on motor torpedo boats was prohibited by the Treaty of Versailles, but the Germans remembered this experience with petrol engines and when the first Schnellbooten were built, less inflammable diesel engines were used as soon as they could be developed.

The most successful use of motor torpedo boats in World War I was by the Italians, who had figured so prominently in motor boat racing before the war. The MAS-boats built by the SVAN yard in Venice were between 50 and 70 feet in length and carried two or four torpedoes at speeds up to 33 knots. The name of these craft actually stood for motor anti-submarine boats, but in fact they were mostly used against surface vessels, particularly Austrian shipping in Adriatic ports. Their most notable successes were the sinking of the old battleship *Wien* at Trieste in December 1917 and the dreadnought *Szent Istvan* in the Straits of Otranto in June 1918.

WORLD WAR II LINE-UP

As far as Britain and the USA were concerned, for most of the period between the wars the attitude of the naval authorities generally was to return to their earlier neglect of motor torpedo boat development, in spite of the successes such craft had achieved in World War I. This was not the case in Germany, however, one reason being that the Versailles Treaty limited the size and number of other vessels that could be built. For instance, when the Germans began to reconstruct their fleet in the mid-1920s, destroyers were limited to no more than 900 tons. Motor torpedo boats were actually banned under the Treaty, but this was overcome by calling them submarine destroyers. Again the Lürssen yard figured prominently in this development. Early in 1928, Lürssen built a luxury motor yacht, the *Oheka II*, for an American client, powered by three 550 hp Maybach engines which gave a speed of over 30 knots and made the yacht reputedly the world's fastest. The Naval High Command obtained the plans from Lürssen and ordered a craft of the same basic design, but with a top speed of 37 knots, and fitted with torpedo-tubes on the forecastle which could be rapidly set up or removed in order to deceive any curious visitors to the yard. The boat, the first Schnellboot – *S.1* – was completed in August 1930 although for reasons of secrecy it was originally commissioned as *UZ (S) .16*. It displaced 39 tons and had an overall length of 29 metres, a beam of 4.5 metres, and draught of 1.6 metres. It was of round-bilge design, which the authorities had found preferable after experiments with the Thornycroft type of planing hull. Armament consisted of two 21inch torpedo tubes forward, one 20mm AA gun and one machine-gun. Grooves in the hull which were necessary to enable the torpedoes to clear the hull when fired were made to look like part of the streamlining. Three Daimler petrol engines of 900 hp each gave a speed of 32 knots. This was less than had been required, but in any case the authorities were not happy with petrol-driven engines, constituting as they did an ever-present fire and explosion hazard. At that time, however, there were no diesel engines available with the necessary power. Contracts for the development of such engines were given to Daimler-Benz in Stuttgart and Maschinen-fabrik Augsburg-Nürnberg (MAN).

Under the command of Oberleutnant Ewerth, *S.1* was given extensive trials, as a result of which various modifications were made, including an enclosed wheelhouse to replace the original open steering position. Four

The English Channel and North Sea

more boats were built by Lürssen in 1932 – *S.2* to *S.5* – with a heavier displacement of 45 tons. These were also constructed of several skins of mahogany on light metal frames and power still had to come from the Daimler petrol engines, although an increase in the rating to 950 hp raised the speed to 35 knots. An important new feature was the addition of a 100 hp Maybach engine, coupled to the centre shaft, which not only increased endurance but also provided a silent-running speed of about 6 knots with the main engines switched off. The crew's quarters (for 1 officer and 13 ratings) were improved to ensure year-round operations, and the new boats were formed into the 1st E-boat Half-Flotilla under the command of Kapitänleutnant Erich Bey. A former 820-ton minesweeper, the *Nordsee*, was converted into a tender to serve as accommodation and depot ship.

Experience with these craft showed them to have only limited seaworthiness, with a tendency for the bows to dip deep in bad weather. This was partly overcome by fitting the next series – *S.6* to *S.13* – with a new bow-form, including a knuckle, while the displacement was increased to 78 tons and the overall dimensions to a length of 32.4 metres, beam of 4.9 metres, and draught of 1.7 metres. The armament was the same as for the earlier boats but the crew was increased to 16-20. *S.6* to *S.9* were fitted with three of the newly-developed MAN diesel engines of 1,320 hp each, but the engines were heavier than intended and limited maximum speed to 32 knots. On the other hand, more success was achieved with the new Daimler diesels of similar horse power, which were fitted in *S.10* to *S.13*. In 1934 a special depot ship, the *Tsingtau* of 1,980 tons, was commissioned to take the place of the old *Nordsee*, and by the following year, with the new boats, it was possible to form the first full-size flotilla. In 1936 five boats, *S.1.* to *S.5.* were taken out of service and sold to Spain.

S.80 series
Displacement: 82 tons
Dimensions: 108 ft x 16 ft x 6 ft
Engines: 3 Daimler Benz diesels of 1,600 bhp each
Maximum speed: 36 knots
Endurance: 800 miles at 30 knots
Armament: 2 x 1 21inch torpedoes, 2 x 1 20mm AA guns
Crew: 16

S.100 series
Displacement: 100 tons
Dimensions: 115 ft x 16½ ft x 6½ ft
Engines: 3 Daimler Benz diesels of 2,000 bhp each
Maximum speed: 42 knots
Endurance: 700 miles at 30 knots
Armament: 2 x 1 21inch torpedoes, 2 x 1 20mm AA guns; later development included 4 x 1 21inch torpedoes and either 1 x 1 40mm AA and 3 x 1 20mm or 1 x 1 37mm AA and 5 x 1 20mm or 3 x 2 30mm AA
Crew: 23

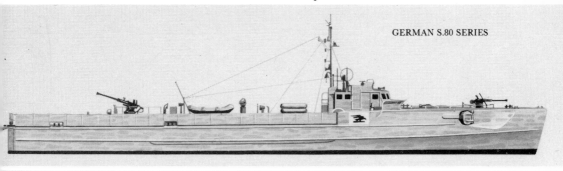

GERMAN S.80 SERIES

GERMAN S.100 SERIES

A further improvement in speed to 37 knots was made possible in the next series – *S.14* to *S.17* commissioned between 1936 and 1938 – by the development of the more powerful 2,000 hp 11-cylinder MAN diesel engine. This was in spite of the fact that displacement was now increased to 97 tons, overall length to 34.62 metres, and beam to 5.26 metres. However, whereas the earlier Daimler-Benz diesels performed without trouble in the heaviest seas, the new MAN engines were very disappointing. As well as causing frequent breakdowns, vibration led to the fracturing of the steel base-plates of the lightly built craft. Eventually it was decided not to use any more MAN engines, and from that point onwards, Daimler-Benz provided all the engines for E-boats. This decision was vindicated by the great success of the next Daimler engine, of 2,000 hp with 20 cylinders in V-form, which powered series *S.18* to *S.25* and was ultimately adopted as the standard E-boat engine.

Because of the more widespread use of light metals and plywood linings these craft, although having the same dimensions as the previous series, were lighter with a displacement of 85 tons. Top speeds of 40 knots were now by no means exceptional.

In August 1938 a second E-boat Flotilla was formed at Wilhelmshaven under the command of Kapitänleutnant Rudolf Petersen. Commander of the 1st Flotilla, based at Kiel, was now Kapitänleutnant Kurt Sturm. And this was the position on the outbreak of World War II, with 18 E-boats in service (*S.24* and *S.25* were delivered later) and more on order. It was not a large force, but over a period of nine years the crews had been able to undergo exhaustive training with their craft, including long non-stop voyages to test the performance and endurance of both men and

British Power Boat Co MGB

Displacement: 47 tons
Dimensions: 71¾ ft x 20½ ft x 5¾ ft
Engines: 3 supercharged Packard of 1,350 bhp each
Maximum speed: 42 knots
Endurance: 600 miles at 15 knots
Armament: 1 x 1 2pdr Pom-Pom, 1 x 1 20mm, 2 x 2 .303 inch machine-guns, 2 depth charges
Crew: 12

BRITISH POWER BOAT
COMPANY MGB 75

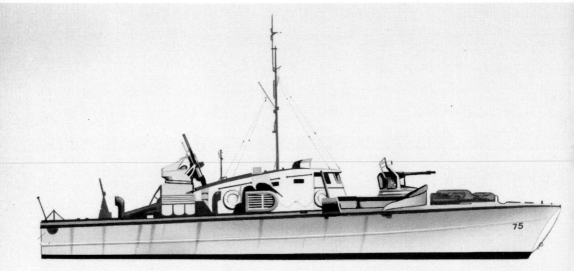

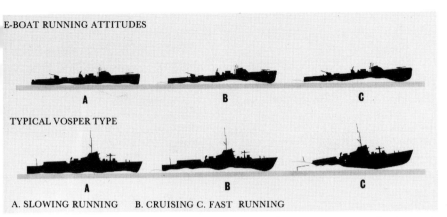

E-BOAT RUNNING ATTITUDES

A   B   C

TYPICAL VOSPER TYPE

A   B   C

A. SLOWING RUNNING   B. CRUISING C. FAST RUNNING

These illustrations show one of the major differences in design between the hard-chine planing hull of the British and American boats, and the round-bilge displacement hull of the German E-boats. The planing hull was more or less mandatory in order to achieve high speed with a short boat, but although it gave inherent lateral stability it did restrict speed in rough weather because of slamming of the flat bottom as the bows lifted out of the water. Another disadvantage was the high plume of water created in the wake which could be seen from miles away at night. The German boats on the other hand remained nearly horizontal even at a top speed which certainly matched and sometimes was higher than the Allied craft. This was partly due to the sheer power of the DaimlerBenz diesel engines, but another factor was the special Lürssen-designed rudder arrangement. Each boat had one main and two side rudders. By steering with the main and turning the side ones outwards to an angle of 30 degrees, an air-filled hollow space (cavitation effect) was created behind the three propellers. This not only improved speed and efficiency, but also reduced the high stern wave and kept the boat almost horizontal at high speed.

machines. As a result of peace-time exercises it was apparent that attack by night offered the best chance of success, with an undetected approach on silent-running motor preferable to a fast but noisy approach using all engines. A grey-white paint was found to provide the best camouflage, surprisingly perhaps, but even on the darkest nights with a phosphorescent sea the boats were barely discernible.

All in all the two E-boat flotillas were in a reasonably good state to go to war. The boats had been thoroughly tested, the crews trained, and some knowledge had been acquired of the tactics that were likely to prove successful. This was in marked contrast to the unprepared situation which existed in Britain.

Soon after the end of World War I, most of the British CMBs were either scrapped or sold and official interest in motor torpedo boats waned. It was not only that the Royal Navy, together with the other Services, was hampered by a lack of funds. Once again there was a tendency in Admiralty circles to think only in terms of big ships at the expense of smaller ones and to forget the danger that had been so apparent in World War I of an enemy basing his maritime policy on the use of mines and torpedoes. However, some work did go ahead on the design of faster and better craft, mainly due to motor boat enthusiasts and men like Hubert Scott-Paine and Commander Peter du Cane who understood the importance of coastal waters. It was not until 1935 that the Admiralty placed its first orders for MTBs, as they were now called, with Scott-Paine's British Power Boat Company. Unlike the round-bilge displacement craft being built by the Germans, Scott-Paine's basic design for a 60-foot MTB called for a hard-chine planing hull. This was virtually mandatory in order to achieve high speeds with a short boat. Although it did give inherent lateral stability, it severely restricted speed in rough weather because of waves slamming the flat bottom, and the high plume of water created astern was another disadvantage as it could be seen from miles away at night. Nevertheless, this design had a lasting influence on most British and American boats built during the war.

The Admiralty purchased six BPB boats to begin with, each powered by three 500 hp Napier petrol engines giving a top speed of 33 knots and armed with two 18inch torpedoes and .303inch machine-guns fore and aft. These were formed into the 1st MTB Flotilla under the command of Lt-Cdr G.B. Sayer and sent to the Mediterranean in 1937, where they were based in Malta. They impressed the Admiralty by making the voyage under their own power in spite of rough weather and orders were placed for twelve more. Six were shipped to Hong Kong as the 2nd MTB Flotilla. The remaining boats were intended to go to Singapore but as they had only reached the Mediterranean by the summer of 1939, when war seemed inevitable, they were allocated instead to the 1st MTB Flotilla to bring its numbers up to twelve.

With the Admiralty showing more interest in small craft towards the end of the 1930s, other British boat-builders began to compete for orders. Two MTBs were designed and constructed as private ventures, one a 68-foot craft by Commander du Cane's Vosper company and the other a larger 70-foot Scott-Paine boat, powered by Rolls-Royce engines. The contest between the two companies was eventually decided in favour of Vosper, whose designs became the basis of most of the short MTBs used by the Royal Navy during the war (as distinct from long MTBs which were over 100 feet in length). However, the first of these boats did not become available until 1940. At the time war broke out, there were only 18 MTBs actually in service with the Royal Navy, twelve of them in Malta and six in Hong Kong. In fact, this was precisely the same number as in German service, but there any similarity ended. The German boats were more heavily armed, with 20mm AA guns as against .303inch machine-guns; their crews were better trained; and they had a distinct advantage in engines which not only gave higher speeds but, being diesels, were far less likely to catch fire if hit than the British petrol-driven motors.

Conscious of her success with motor torpedo boats during World War I, Italy did more than any other country to continue development of these craft in the inter-war period. When World War II began, the Italian Navy had nearly 100 boats in service. They were generally smaller than those being built in Britain, Germany or the USA, having been designed for use in the calmer waters of the Mediterranean and Adriatic rather than the North Sea. Overall length ranged from 48 feet, displacing 12 tons, to 60 feet displacing 26 tons. One great advantage was the Isotta-Fraschini marine petrol engine, probably the best of its kind in the world at that time, which gave the Italian craft speeds of up to 45 knots and made them faster than any other boats then in service.

Even in 1929, when the SVAN yard built its first modern motor torpedo boat, the 48-foot 12¾-ton *MAS.423* powered by 1,500 hp Isotta-Fraschini engines and armed with two 6.5mm machine-guns and two 17.7inch torpedoes, a maximum speed of 40 knots was possible. This was the basic design for most of the Italian boats built until the mid-1930s, although speed was increased with the development of more powerful engines and depth charges were also carried for anti-submarine operations. In 1936 the Baglietto yard at Varazze built a larger type, 55 feet in length, armed with one 13.2mm machine-gun, two 17.7inch torpedoes and six depth charges, and also powered by Isotta-Fraschini engines which gave over 42 knots. Boats built to this basic design, with the overall length increased to 60 feet, formed the bulk of the Italian motor torpedo boat fleet at the start of the war.

The US Navy continued to show little interest in motor torpedo boats

Italian MAS boat
Displacement: 66 tons
Dimensions: 28 x 4.3 x 1.6 metres
Engines: 3 Isotta Fraschini, total 3,450 hp
Maximum speed: 34 knots
Armament: 2 x 1 21inch torpedoes, 2 x 1 17.7inch torpedoes aft, 2 to 4 20mm/65, 12 to 20 depth charges
Crew: 19

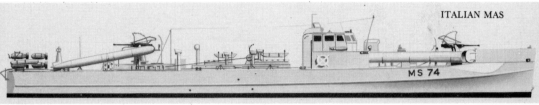

ITALIAN MAS

MS 74

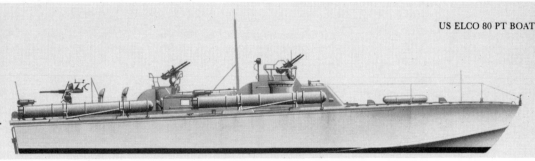

US ELCO 80 PT BOAT

during the inter-war period and it was not until 1937 that President Roosevelt, who as Assistant Secretary of the Navy in World War I had been among the few to appreciate the value of such craft, sponsored an appropriation of $15 million for the development of suitable boats. Prizes were offered to private designers for a number of small-boat designs, and one winner was Sparkman and Stephens, naval architects, with a 70-foot motor torpedo boat. In May 1939, Higgins Industries of New Orleans was given a contract to build two PT-boats based on this design but scaled up to 81 feet. The Navy also began to build several experimental craft of its own. But later in 1939 Scott-Paine, the English designer who had failed to get the Royal Navy's contract for MTBs in competition with Vosper, took his British Power Boat Company's 70-foot craft across the Atlantic and sold it to the US Navy for evaluation. It was soon obvious that the BPB boat was superior to any of the others under consideration and arrangements were made for it to be built under licence in the USA by the Electric Boat Company (Elco). The only major modification was the substitution of 1,200 hp Packard engines for the original Rolls-Royce engines. Scott-Paine's original boat had to be used for taking measurements and it was not until June 1940 that it was finally delivered to the US Navy for

US Elco 80 ft PT boat
Displacement: 38 tons
Dimensions: 80 ft x 20¾ ft x 5 ft
Engines: 3 12-cylinder Packard, originally rated at 1,200 bhp each but progressively increased to 1,350 and finally 1,500
Maximum speed: 40 knots
Endurance: 500 miles at 20 knots
Armament: 4 x 1 18inch torpedoes, 2 x 2 .5inch machine-guns: later developments included 4 x 1 21inch torpedoes, 2 x 1 20mm, 1 x 1 37mm or 2 x 1 40mm, and finally experiments with 75mm, 4.5inch barrage rocket projectors, and 5inch spin-stabilized rockets
Crew: 14

operational use as *PT.9* – the first American patrol torpedo boat. (*PTs. 1-8* were experimental craft still under construction; none of them ultimately proved to be very satisfactory.)

Meanwhile, Higgins had been working on modifications to the boats it had been contracted to build, and in February 1941 delivered a new 78-foot craft which proved to be highly satisfactory during its trials. The Navy had already called for modifications to the Elco boats to make them bigger in order to carry four 21inch torpedoes, and eventually settled on two standard types of boat, the Elco 80-footer (38 tons) and the Higgins 78-footer (35 tons). Both were powered by three Packard marine petrol engines, originally rated at 1,200 hp but later increased to 1,350 hp and finally to 1,500 hp as the boats increased in weight with heavier armament. Many changes had been made but both boats owed much to the original Scott-Paine design, with a hard-chine stepless bottom hull and outward flaring of the sides. They were designed for top speeds of at least 40 knots and a cruising range of 500 miles. The Elco boat was slightly faster but the Higgins was more manoeuvrable, so that crews were divided as to which was considered best. Four torpedo tubes were installed, for 18inch torpedoes to begin with, later increased to 21inch, and the first boats to enter service were armed with two twin .5inch machine-guns.

The major power which did the least in motor torpedo boat development before World War II was Japan, concentrating her efforts on building the bigger warships that had been denied to the nation in the 1920s and early 1930s by various Naval Treaties. In 1938, however, the Japanese captured a Thornycroft CMB at Canton and from this the Tsurumi yard developed an experimental craft. This led to the *T.I.* type, seven of which were built, entering service in 1941 as the Navy's only motor torpedo boats. They were 59 feet in length, powered by two petrol engines of 1,800 hp which gave a speed of about 35 knots, and armed with two 18inch torpedoes, or six depth charges, and two 7.7mm machine-guns.

Vosper 72½ ft MTB
Displacement: 40 tons
Dimensions: 72½ ft x 19¼ ft x 6¼ ft
Engines: 3 supercharged Packard of 1,400 bhp each
Maximum speed: 39 knots
Endurance: 400 miles at 20 knots
Armament: 2 x 1 21inch torpedoes, 2 depth charges, 1 x 2 .5inch and 2 x 1 .303inch machine-guns; later development included 1 x 2 20mm and 1 x 1 2pdr forward
Crew: 13

VOSPER MTB

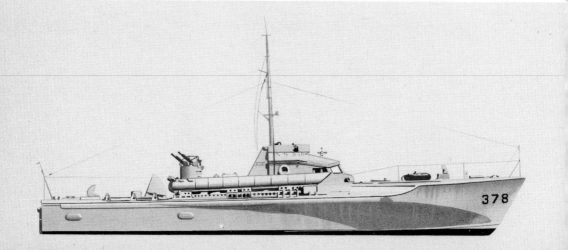

MERCHANT SHIPPING UNDER ATTACK

The E-Boat threat to Britain's coastal shipping during World War II has to be seen in the context both of other weapons also used for this purpose and of the maritime strategies employed by Britain and Germany. In August 1939, the Merchant Navy of the British Empire totalled 9,448 vessels of over 21 million tons. Registered in Britain were some 3,000 deep-sea dry cargo ships and tankers and about 1,000 coasting vessels, the latter shipping goods and materials from one part of the country to another along the east coast. This was a vital task since the inland transportation system, by road or rail, could not have coped with such an amount of traffic. At any one time between two and three hundred vessels were likely to be sailing up and down this route. As far as the total merchant fleet was concerned, some 2,500 ships would be at sea on any one day, with ocean-going cargo vessels and tankers bringing supplies into Britain from all over the world.

Ever since 1936, when Hitler's march into the Rhineland showed the British Chiefs-of-Staff at least that war with Germany was likely to become inevitable (they even predicted in a memorandum to the Cabinet that it would break out in the latter part of 1939), the Royal Navy had been considering plans to protect this shipping. Of necessity, the war plans adopted by the Admiralty in January 1939 were based on a defensive strategy, to allow time for a sufficient force to be built up and trained for the offensive. The first priority was the defence of trade in home waters and the Atlantic, both fundamental to Britain's ability to fight the war. Secondly, there was the defence of trade in the Mediterranean and Indian Ocean, without which shipping would be forced to take the longer route round the Cape of Good Hope. And the third broad part of the naval plan was to impose a blockade on Germany and Italy, preventing shipments into the two countries even if carried in neutral ships.

It is primarily with the first of these objectives that this book is concerned. While the main part of the Home Fleet was stationed at Scapa Flow, ready to meet any major surface threat which the enemy could mount at sea, four naval shore commands were established – Portsmouth, the Nore (Chatham), the Western Approaches (Plymouth) and Rosyth – with the responsibility of controlling coastal waters and defending the merchant shipping that was being funnelled into British ports from all over the world. Each command had forces of destroyers, anti-submarine vessels and minesweepers which, based on the existing naval knowledge of that time, seemed sufficient to give adequate protection. It was recognised that the convoy system provided the best protection against enemy submarine and air attacks, but the Royal Navy's cruiser-strength was not sufficient to enable ocean convoys to be formed at once. Instead, therefore, the Admiralty intended to patrol certain focal areas through which most shipping had to pass and to rely on 'evasive routing' to enable ships to sail independently from one area to another. Plans were made for the Admiralty to assume control of all merchant shipping as soon as war seemed probable, and in fact the necessary orders were made on 26 August 1939.

It was obvious that the first impact of German submarine warfare, air attacks and minelaying would be felt in home waters and the sea approaches to Britain, and plans to combat these threats were made accordingly. A start was made on equipping all ocean-going merchant ships, coastal vessels, and some fishing boats and smaller craft with low-angle anti-submarine guns and high-angle anti-aircraft machine-

Prior to sailing, the captains of all the ships taking part in a British East Coast convoy meet to receive instructions from the escort commander, including course, positions in convoy, and the latest situation as regards swept channels through minefields

guns, although there was a woeful shortage of suitable weapons. (Under the rules of International Law, deck guns could not be trained to fire forward of the beam as this was considered offensive as against merely defensive.) The Strait of Dover was to be closed and the passage of U-boats by the shortest route to the Atlantic blocked by laying a mine barrage across the narrows. A powerful squadron of warships called the Channel Force was based at Portland to guard the approaches to the English Channel and the Irish Sea from the west, while to deal with any attempt by the Germans to operate light forces in the southern part of the North Sea, a cruiser squadron and destroyer flotilla were detached from the Home Fleet and based on the Humber.

The east coast shipping from Scotland and the Tyne to the Thames was particularly exposed to attack. Since it was not possible for all ships to be diverted to the west coast, convoys with escorts were to be run from the outset in both directions between Southend and Methil on the Firth of Forth. To guard against U-boats or surface ships, a minefield was to be laid in several stages along most of the convoy route.

It was not until early 1939, and rather belatedly, that serious consideration was given to the vulnerability of east coast shipping to air attack. At that time, pilots were not trained in sea-air co-operation, since this was not within the responsibilities of RAF Fighter Command, and control from the ground could not be extended more than a few miles from the shore. In the summer of that eventful year, four Trade Protection Squadrons of Blenheim fighters were approved for allocation to Fighter Command. However, these were not actually formed until after the outbreak of war, and serious losses were suffered from enemy air attack until air protection was properly organised.

Germany's war plans were, of course, coloured by the fact that her fleet was basically unprepared for war, since Hitler had told Admiral Raeder that he would not precipitate a general war until 1944. It was on that assumption that German naval expansion had been planned, and when war broke out, many ships were still building or at the planning stage. Nevertheless, the German Navy still comprised a powerful force, in particular 56 U-boats of which all but ten were operational, with highly trained crews. The German battle instructions issued in May 1939 ordered a continuous series of operations in the North Sea, mainly attacks on shipping to create as much nuisance as possible and thus tying down large British forces to contain them. All the larger ships were to cruise the oceans in a sustained attack on merchant shipping. The ocean-going U-boats were to operate against trade in the Atlantic and the approaches to British ports while the smaller coastal type were given the task of laying mines off the Channel ports. In order to make up partly for the delay in the new heavy ships still under construction, a number of merchant ships were taken over for conversion into fast, heavily-armed raiders.

In relegating operations in the North Sea to 'constant harassing action',

A convoy forms up outside port before taking the East Coast route some time in 1942. It includes small mercantile vessels equipped with barrage balloons to protect the convoy from dive-bomber and strafing attacks, part of a force that began forming in July 1940 and was based on Sheerness

the Germans were accepting that their naval forces were not strong enough to attempt to obtain naval supremacy. They admitted that their forces would be excluded from the Channel in a very short time and held out little hope of adequately protecting their own coastal shipping in the North Sea. As actual events were to prove, the Germans probably underestimated their capabilities and did not sufficiently appreciate the weaknesses of the British. Although the Royal Navy was numerically superior, many of its ships dated back to World War I whereas most of the German ships were new. Some of the British naval bases, even Scapa Flow, did not have adequate anti-aircraft defences, which could have been exploited more by the Germans. However, a major factor in the early stages of the war was that both sides underestimated the importance of air power at sea.

Within hours of the declaration of war, the Royal Navy had to revise its plans drastically with the sinking of the liner *Athenia* by a U-boat 200 miles west of the Hebrides. Although the captain of *U.30* exceeded his instructions in sinking a civilian ship, it was certainly in line with the cynical German battle order that 'fighting methods will never fail to be employed merely because some international regulations are opposed to them.' The British Admiralty took the loss of the *Athenia* as evidence that the Germans intended to wage unrestricted submarine warfare from the beginning. In view of this the Admiralty decided to abandon the 'evasive routing' of merchant ships and to adopt the full convoy system. The only trouble was a lack of sufficient escort vessels to make this immediately possible. Due to the lateness of the pre-war naval rebuilding programme the destroyers

and other vessels available as convoy escorts lacked the endurance to take them far into the Atlantic. Until new high-endurance ships were built, a 'limit of convoy' had to be established at a point about 300 miles to the west, after which convoys were dispersed and ships proceeded independently. Incoming convoys were escorted across the Atlantic by an escort, usually an armed merchant cruiser, and then picked up by other escort forces at the limit of convoy and brought into British ports. This limit was pushed further westwards as new ships became available, but it was not until mid-1941 that the Royal Navy could provide anti-submarine escort all the way across the Atlantic.

Meanwhile, the first east coast convoy started on 6 September 1939, only three days after the declaration of war. This was in fact the earliest use of the mercantile convoy system defined as running at regular intervals from the same port of assembly. Initially the convoys sailed in each direction every second day, with the designation FN followed by a number for the northward voyage from the Thames to the Firth of Forth and FS followed by a number for the voyage back. These convoys were the special responsibility of the Rosyth Escort Force, whose ships had anti-aircraft as well as anti-submarine armament. On 7 September the first outward-bound ocean convoys started, one series sailing every alternate day down-Channel from Southend and another leaving Liverpool, generally on the same day, and sailing south through the Irish Sea. During the early stages of the war, destroyers provided close escort for only 300 miles into the Atlantic. After this, the west-bound ships dispersed and continued indepently while those south-bound were formed into Gibraltar

An East Coast convoy at sea, taken from HM Trawler Sapphire; such vessels, usually armed with a 4-inch or 12-pounder AA gun (as here), performed a variety of essential escort tasks, such as rounding up stragglers, standing by damaged ships, or even towing them to the nearest port if they were disabled

convoys with one ocean escort until they were met by anti-submarine vessels from Gibraltar. The close escort destroyers usually waited at the rendezvous point to bring back the next inward convoy. The first of the famous Halifax convoys, around which the Battle of the Atlantic was

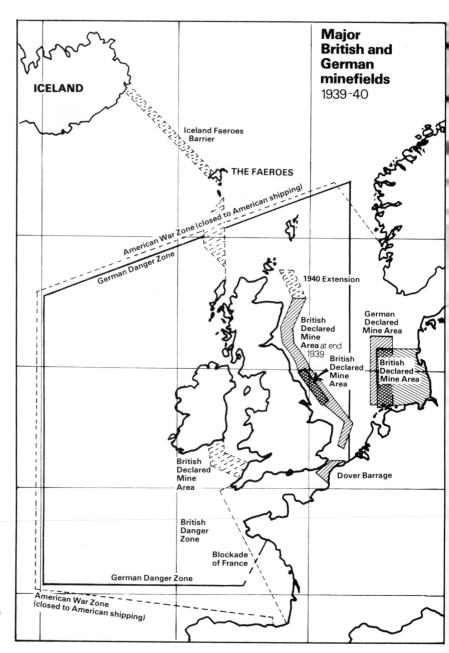

Major British and German minefields 1939~40

ICELAND

Iceland Faeroes Barrier

THE FAEROES

American War Zone (closed to American shipping)

German Danger Zone

1940 Extension

British Declared Mine Area at end 1939

British Declared Mine Area

German Declared Mine Area

British Declared Mine Area

British Declared Mine Area

Dover Barrage

British Danger Zone

Blockade of France

German Danger Zone

American War Zone (closed to American shipping)

German Mine (BMC)
1943/44
Charge 1430 lb

largely to revolve, set sail under Canadian local escort on 16 September.

The earliest U-boat successes were against merchant ships already on their way to Britain but sailing independently, either because they had not yet been brought into the convoy system or because they were able to steam within certain ranges of speed over 15 knots in the North Atlantic or below 9 knots generally – in which case it was not intended that they should join convoys. By the end of 1939, U-boats had sunk 114 British, Allied and Neutral merchant ships, with a total tonnage of 421,156, but this included only four out of 5,756 convoyed ships, proving the value of the system. Nine U-boats had been sunk, and considering the limited number of escort vessels available, the figures were fairly encouraging. However, there was plenty to worry about when looking into the future. It was known that Germany was already building a substantial number of U-boats, which could double or treble the total by 1941 with progressive increases as the war continued. Also, attempts to take the offensive against U-boats by forming warships into hunting groups had ended in disaster, with the sinking of the aircraft carrier *Courageous* by *U.29*. After that, the Admiralty wisely decided it was too risky to use such ships for that type of warfare.

Within days of the declaration of war, the Royal Navy began to carry out the Admiralty's war plan by laying a defensive mine barrier in the English Channel. The first stage was completed by 12 September and in October, when three U-boats were destroyed by mines in that area, the Germans gave up any attempt to send coastal submarines by the shortest route to the Western approaches. It was also intended to lay minefields offshore the east coast convoy route, some twenty miles wide and a similar distance from shore, but work was not in fact started on this until the following year. However, the Germans were also busy with minelaying operations in these waters right from the start, initially laying mines from submarines. The first ship to be mined in the war was the British steamer *Magdepur*, which blew up and sank off the east coast on 10 September. Within the next few weeks the losses due to mines had risen to serious proportions, and not all of them easily explained. Hitler had boasted of a 'secret weapon' he intended to employ against British shipping, and by piecing together all the available evidence, including statements by a prisoner-of-war, it became apparent that the Germans were using magnetic mines.

The type of mine generally used at that time by both sides was the contact variety, moored to the seabed so that it floated just under the surface of the sea and required actual contact with a ship's hull to detonate the explosive. The Germans, however, had developed and put into production the first of a long series of mines known as the influence type which did not require actual contact with a passing ship but exploded through some other 'influence' – a ship's magnetic field in the case of the magnetic mine. This was by no means a new weapon; the Royal

German mine (EMF)
1939/41/42
Buoyant with influence firing

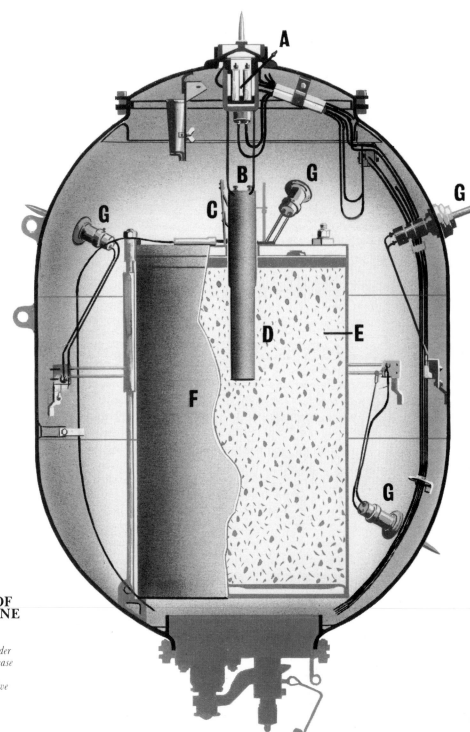

**KEY TO
DIAGRAM OF
BRITISH MINE
MARK XV**

A   *Battery*
B   *Detonator Holder*
C   *Detonator Release*
D   *Primer*
E   *500 lb Explosive
       Charge*
F   *Charge Case*
G   *Switch Horns*

Navy had used a similar type off the Belgian coast during World War I, although it was not successful, and after development along somewhat different lines was ready in 1939 to go into production with a standard magnetic mine. One problem from Britain's point of view was that it was impossible to know which of all the numerous variations in magnetic influence the Germans had employed for exploding the mines. Another was that the mines were laid on the seabed and could not be swept by any existing device since Britain's entire minesweeping force, as well as additional equipment planned and ordered, was designed only to deal with moored contact mines.

There was no way of solving either problem without studying a specimen mine and discovering its mechanism. By the end of October most of the 19 ships of 59,027 tons that had been lost through mines were sunk by the five magnetic fields laid off the east coast and in the Thames estuary, and the situation was becoming serious. When, in mid-November, the Germans started dropping mines from aircraft, this seemed only to add to the problem. For a while it was feared that the flow of traffic in and out of the Port of London might be stopped entirely. But ironically, this new approach led to the eventual solution. On 23 November, a Heinkel 115 was seen to drop a mine by parachute on the mudflats off Shoeburyness on the Thames estuary. At great personal risk, a team led by Lieutenant-Commander J.G.D. Ouvry RN defused the mine. It was sent to the Mine Experimental Department at HMS *Vernon* where it was stripped down and all its secrets laid bare. It was discovered that the magnetic needle which detonated the explosive became active through a change of magnetism (as distinct from the rate of change in the British mine) in the vertical (as opposed to the horizontal) field, and that it was designed to be operative against ships built in the northern hemisphere which had their north magnetic poles downwards.

Now the problem could at last be passed to the scientists. A new magnetic sweep was developed, and used both by ships and specially converted Wellington aircraft, for exploding the mines harmlessly and thereby clearing paths through enemy minefields. Also, British and Allied vessels were equipped with a simple but effective 'degaussing girdle', a band of wire fastened round the hull, level with the upper deck and energised by an electric current, which had the effect of neutralising the ship's magnetism and providing almost complete immunity. At one time, 1,200 miles of wire cable a week were being used to fit the ships. It was ironic that the unit of magnetic flux, one of the means of countering the magnetic mine, should derive its name from a German scientist, Carl Frederick Gauss (1777-1855).

Although the general outlook became less critical due to these efforts, the pressure was very severe on the minesweepers of Nore Command, especially in December when the Germans switched their minelaying activities from the Thames estuary to the narrow channels off the Norfolk

German Mine (FMC)
with sinker box
90 lb charge

coast through which the east coast convoys had to pass. From the start of their offensive minelaying campaign the Germans were, of course, contravening the Hague Conventions by laying mines wherever they were likely to achieve results and not confining them to declared areas, but this was only one of the illegalities being practised. By the end of the year, 79 British, Allied and Neutral merchant ships totalling 262,697 tons had been lost through mines, more in fact than from enemy warships (51 vessels of 61,337 tons) or from aircraft (ten ships of 2,949 tons), and second only to U-boats. It was clear that this form of warfare was a major factor to be taken into account. For the rest of the war there was a fluctuating battle between minelaying and minesweeping as scientists on both sides strove to develop new types of mine, giving their opposite numbers the problem of unravelling their secrets in order to find a means of combating them. The next phase in the battle began in the spring of 1940 when, with the German occupation of Norway, Denmark, Holland, Belgium and France, E-boats came into the picture, used both for laying mines and for torpedo attacks on the east coast convoys.

E-BOATS IN ACTION

Shortly before the outbreak of war the 1st E-boat Flotilla was ordered into the Baltic to patrol the Gulf of Danzig, and it was here, within the first hour after hostilities were opened, that the first success was achieved when *S.23* sank a small Polish pilot vessel by gunfire. Meanwhile, the 2nd Flotilla began patrols in the northern North Sea, using Heligoland as a base. But rough seas damaged several of the boats, including *S.17* which had to be withdrawn from service, and the onset of an early, hard winter put paid to large-scale operations. At the end of November the 1st Flotilla was ordered back to Kiel. Here it became iced-in, so that boats could only be moved by hacking the surrounding ice with axes and picks. This was still the situation in mid-March 1940, when it was decided that the two flotillas should take part in 'Operation Weserübung', the German occupation of Denmark and Norway. After carefully considering the problem of the boats trapped in Kiel, protective steel plates were fitted around their propellers and rudders, then ice-breakers led the way for them down the Kiel Canal to the port of Wilhelmshaven and the open waters of the North Sea.

During the winter, meanwhile, new boats had been completed and sent to Kiel for fitting out. With *S.26* came a new Lürssen design which was the basis for all E-boats built during the war. The most notable changes were that the forecastle was closed in and covered with a cupola-shaped bridge, and the two forward 20inch torpedo tubes were built into the hull below the forecastle deck. Hinged flaps at the front remained closed until the torpedoes were to be fired. This design gave the boats their distinctive low and lean shape and contributed considerably to their seaworthiness and speed. Ninety-three of this series were to be built over the next three years, with only slight modifications. Their performance was an improvement on the previous craft, with a top speed of 40 knots and a range of 700 miles at a cruising speed of 30 knots. The crew was kept at 21 but displacement was increased from 85 to 100 tons, partly due to the new design and also to the two spare torpedoes carried in chocks on a level with and immediately behind the torpedo tubes. Armament remained at two 20mm anti-aircraft guns for the time being. Most of these boats were built by Lürssen although a few came from the Schlichting yard at Travemünde. As they were brought into service and formed into new flotillas, so new depot ships were built, the 2,900-ton *Carl Peters* being the first of five to be commissioned in 1940.

For the operation against Bergen, the 1st Flotilla with its tender *Carl Peters* was assigned to Naval Task Force III, which also included the cruisers *Köln* and *Königsberg* and two torpedo boats. The 2nd Flotilla, including some of the new craft and its tender *Tsingtaù*, was to assist the cruiser *Karlsruhe* and three torpedo boats as Naval Task Force IV in the capture of Kristiansand. At this time all E-boats were under the naval command SO Torpedoboats, and it was not until April 1942 that they were formed into a separate command of their own. The two flotillas set out from their bases on the evening of 8 April. As they neared the Norwegian coast the sea began to get rough and the commanders had difficulty keeping formation. Two boats of the 1st Flotilla actually collided and had to be towed back to port. One of them was commanded by Kapitänleutnant Siegfried Wuppermann, later to become the best-known 'ace' commander in the Mediterranean theatre.

Following the successful landing in Norway, during which the E-boats shuttled troops of the Wehrmacht ashore, they were employed to reconnoitre the numerous fjords, hunting for hidden Norwegian vessels whose captains hoped to make a break for the open sea. It was during this period that boats of the 1st Flotilla sank the Norwegian torpedo boat *Sael*, but the flotilla itself suffered considerable damage at various times from air attack and heavy machine-gun fire from the shore.

At the end of April, while the 1st Flotilla remained off Norway as the only active German naval presence in the area following the withdrawal of the cruisers and torpedo boats, Peterson's 2nd Flotilla was ordered back to Wilhelmshaven. Here the boats were ordered to undertake operations in the English Channel. The German offensive against the Low Countries and France was about to begin, presenting the E-boats with their first major challenge as an offensive weapon in the open seas. The voyage from Wilhelmshaven to the Channel was a distance of some 200 miles, which had to be repeated again on the return to base, and no-one quite knew what to expect. E-boats had never operated so far from base before. The general orders from Naval High Command were that they should attack British shipping in the area. On the night of 9th May four boats set out on the first sortie, under the command of Peterson in *S.30*. They were to patrol the north-east of the Dover Strait.

At 22.00 hours the commander of *S.32*, Lt. Kosky, sighted shadows on the horizon. Drawing nearer, he recognised the familiar outline of British destroyers – the 2nd Flotilla had in fact run into a force of cruisers and destroyers of Home Command that was searching for German minelayers. Peterson ordered the boats to circle eastwards, quietly on single engines, so that they could attack from the dark horizon. But as they were creeping nearer, they were suddenly sighted. A light signalled from one of the destroyers. Peterson was unable to reply with the correct identification. Seconds later the destroyers began firing. Vivid flashes lit the night sky, while the sea around the E-boats boiled with falling shells.

With an ear-splitting roar the engines of the E-boats were crash-started. The boats heeled to port and at 40 knots, with bows lifting from the water, they sped out of range of the destroyers' guns. In the confusion, however, the boats lost contact with each other. Peterson and Kosky both found they were running dangerously low on fuel and were compelled to set off on the long haul home. The crew of *S.33* found themselves in a fog bank and were just congratulating themselves that they had escaped to safety when a huge grey shadow loomed ahead of them.

'It was another of the British destroyers,' the commander later

THE NORTH SEA

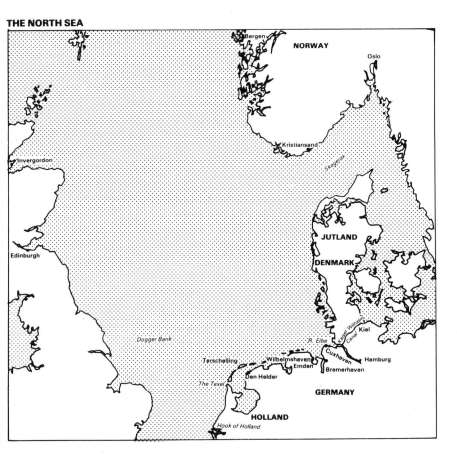

reported. 'We were unable to turn in time and crashed straight into her. Our bow scraped along her flank and eventually came free. But before we had overcome our fear there was another crash and we collided with her stern. All this time the destroyer's guns had been firing, not at us but simply in any direction. They must have been as nervous as we were.'

The destroyer steamed away and *S.33* was left alone, its crew expecting to sink at any moment. But somehow the craft was still making about 15 knots. Not knowing if his boat was seaworthy or not, the commander ordered scuttling charges to be set, then laid a smoke screen and set course for home. Examination showed that the two forward compartments were filled with water, but the most astonishing thing was that a full eighteen feet of the bows and forecastle had simply disappeared, leaving a large jagged hole. The pumps were kept working at full pressure to keep the boat afloat, and in this condition *S.33* managed to complete the 200 miles back to base. Engineers at Wilhelmshaven repair yard were highly impressed with the boat's stability even after the damage sustained, and the incident helped to confirm the value and suitability of E-boats in the mind of Naval High Command.

But the E-boats had even more reason for congratulations. While turning for home the fourth boat in the patrol, *S.31* commanded by Oberleutnant Opdenhoff, found one of the British destroyers dead ahead. What was more, *S.31* was fortunately approaching from the dark horizon and had not been sighted. At a range of 2,400 yards Opdenhoff fired two torpedoes. Only then did the guns of the destroyer open fire, but moments later there were two deafening explosions as the torpedoes struck home. Opdenhoff could not wait to judge their effect but he was convinced the ship would sink and this was announced by German radio the following day. In fact, the torpedoes had hit the destroyer *Kelly* which, although very badly damaged, was taken under tow for 91 hours and successfully brought into the Tyne for extensive repairs.

Nevertheless, this example of what a small boat could do against such a ship came as a shock to the British Admiralty. Worse was to follow. In mid-May the 1st E-boat Flotilla was brought back from Norway to join the 2nd and on the night of 21 May scored its first success by sinking the British Mine Destructor Vessel *Corburn* off Le Havre, followed up two nights later by the sinking of the French destroyer *Jaguar* off Malo-les-Bains. In both instances the E-boats had made their way undetected through the Dover Strait, a passage denied to larger warships and U-boats because of the mine barrage and shore gun batteries. An even greater danger became apparent when, with the German occupation of Holland and Belgium and the imminent fall of France, it was realised that the Germans would have access to bases all along the coast of Western Europe. From here they could attack British coastal shipping without the necessity of a long and difficult voyage from Wilhelmshaven. The first of these E-boat bases was constructed on the island of Borkum on the

Friesland coast; the biggest initial problem was the fine sand which, borne by the constant wind, found its way into the highly sensitive diesel engines with a very damaging effect. This was eventually overcome by planting grass on the sand dunes.

The British Admiralty was forced for the first time to give serious consideration to the threat from the previously despised motor torpedo boats. But MTBs quickly showed that they were not suitable for combating the well-armed E-boats. The first operational MTB base had been formed at Felixstowe on the east coast in January 1940, comprising BPB craft of the 1st MTB Flotilla which had been recalled from Malta two months earlier. But the main contract for MTBs had gone to Vospers and the first of these boats were forming up in Portsmouth into the 4th MTB Flotilla. Based on the experimental boat built in 1937 and selected by the Admiralty the following year after extensive trials, these boats were 70 feet overall, 36 tons, armed with two twin .5inch machine-guns and two 21inch torpedoes carried in tubes. These were 24 feet long and consisted of a 500 lb warhead, a long body containing an air vessel filled to a pressure of 2,500 lbs per square inch, and a tail section comprising an engine, contra-rotating propellers, and horizontal and vertical rudders. Launching was achieved by firing cordite in an impulse chamber at the rear of the tube to produce expanding gases. The depth was pre-set and a torpedo normally ran at just over 40 knots with a range of some 10,000 yards. The warhead armed itself after hitting the water. MTBs usually carried a crew of ten. To begin with they were powered by three Isotta-Fraschini petrol engines giving 3,600 hp and a top speed of just on 40 knots, but supplies naturally ceased when Italy entered the war. Super-charged Hall-Scott engines were used for a time until supplies of Packard engines could be obtained from America, the first arriving in 1941. Thereafter these were used to power virtually all the British boats.

The 4th Flotilla was sent to Felixstowe in May, together with the 3rd and 10th Flotillas which comprised a mixed assortment of Thornycroft, BPB, Vosper and old experimental craft. At this time, MTBs came under the authority of the individual naval home commands. It was not until November 1940 that Coastal Forces was formed as a separate organisation and only in 1943 did it take operational control of MTBs and MGBs, with a department of its own within the Admiralty. To begin with the Commanders-in-Chief, who saw little value in light craft anyway, assigned the MTBs to escorting coastal convoys. Designed to be an offensive and not a defensive weapon, they were of course totally ill-equipped for this task, especially when armed only with .303inch machine-guns which was the case until 20mm Oerlikons became available. They had their torpedoes, of course, but these were of little use against submarines and E-boats, and the Germans wisely decided to employ these weapons rather than larger warships against coastal shipping.

It must be borne in mind that the coastal shipping off Germany was far

nore limited than in Britain's case, so that the MTBs had fewer targets available to them than the E-boats. This changed to some extent when Germany occupied Western Europe and the coastal shipping off France, Belgium and Holland became subject to attack, giving the MTBs more opportunities to take the offensive. Even so, the amount of shipping was never as large as that off Britain's east coast, which makes it invidious to compare the results achieved by motor torpedo boats of the two sides during the war. Another factor bearing on this was Britain's particular problem – a comparative lack of escorts to protect the many merchant ships in service – whereas the Germans had fewer coasters and consequently a greater proportion of escort vessels, including destroyers, torpedo boats, armed trawlers and minelayers as well as lighter craft. Thus from the start their E-boats were available to be used in a more aggressive role.

Ironically, while E-boats were sinking ships up to the size of destroyer, the first success of the MTBs was against an aircraft. On 12 May, in their first operation across the North Sea, three boats of the 3rd Flotilla were sent into action against the enemy in the Zuiderzee, following the German invasion of Holland. There was little they could do except to evacuate a number of refugees and servicemen, and on the afternoon of 14 May they set off to return to Felixstowe. While crossing the North Sea they were attacked by two seaplanes, a Dornier and a Heinkel. Not only were the boats undamaged but the gunner on *MTB.24* succeeded in shooting down the Heinkel while gunners on the two other craft managed to hit and possibly downed the Dornier. The ability of MTBs to use their speed to avoid attack from the air was a noticeable factor two weeks later when all the serviceable craft, together with every other available vessel in Britain, were called upon to take part in the evacuation of the British Expeditionary Force from Dunkirk. They excelled themselves in ferrying troops from the beaches to the larger ships moored offshore, one boat commanded by Lt Stewart Gould being on continuous duty for more than 24 hours under heavy gunfire and only then returning home when damaged. Other MTBs patrolled the eastern flank of the area in an attempt to hold off marauding E-boats, but were unable to prevent *S.30* (Oberleutnant Wilhelm Zimmermann) from sinking the British destroyer *Wakeful*, *S.24* (Oberleutnant Hans Detlefsen) from torpedoing and damaging the French destroyer *Cyclone*, and *S.26* (Oberleutnant Kurt Fimmen) from sinking the *Cyclone*'s sister ship, the *Sirocco*.

These successes only confirmed that fast, more heavily armed gunboats were needed to combat the German craft. The British Power Boat Company was given the task of designing an MGB for that specific duty and eventually came up with a craft that was 71½ feet overall, 47 tons, powered by three Packard engines of 4,050 hp giving 40 knots and armed with one 2-pounder (40mm) gun, one twin 20mm, two twin .303inch machine-guns, and two depth charges. Crew consisted of two officers and

Opposite: A Fairmile 'B' motor launch, built in Canada for the Royal Canadian Navy and used for anti-submarine patrols in the St Lawrence and other rivers and estuaries. Armament comprised a 3-pounder forward, a 20mm Oerlikon amidships and a twin Oerlikon aft, and two twin .303inch machine-guns on pedestals. These MLs also carried 14 depth charges in chutes and a Holman Illuminant projector

A broadside view of a Canadian-built Fairmile 'B' motor launch

ten men. Like the MTBs they had planing hulls of hard-chine double-skin mahogany and were known as 'short' boats (under 100 feet). Another kind of MGB was the 'long' type, based on a 110-foot motor launch designed by Norman Hart before the war. Twelve of these were in service by 1940, mostly built by the Fairmile Marine Company; of prefabricated, hard-chine construction, these MLs were intended for patrol and escort duties off the coast. Their proven seaworthiness led to the development of a modified version for use as motor gunboats, known as the Fairmile 'C' type. These were 110 feet overall, displacing 72 tons, powered by three Hall-Scott petrol engines of 2,700 hp, super-charged to give a speed of up to 27 knots. They were armed with two 2-pounders, two twin .5inch and two twin .303inch machine-guns, and carried a crew of sixteen.

However, these MGBs were not available for service until 1941 in the case of the Fairmile and 1942 for the BPB type. There was an urgent need for some kind of MGB to use during the interim period. Accordingly, the Admiralty looked around for some kind of boat that could be converted for that purpose. In 1932, the BPB Company had begun to build Motor Anti-Submarine Boats (MA/SBs) when it seemed that German submarines might operate in the English Channel. The boats were a twin-screw version of Scott-Paine's 60-foot MTB design which sacrificed speed and torpedoes in favour of depth charges and Asdic equipment. They were powered by two Napier engines of 1,000 bhp which gave a top speed of 25 knots and were only lightly armed with .303inch machine-guns. Six were in service when war broke out, with another 16 of 70 feet overall under construction. It soon became apparent, however, that air patrols and minefields were sufficient to keep most German submarines away from coastal waters, and in any case the MA/SBs did not come up to expectations. This was not primarily the fault of the craft themselves. Before the war, the Admiralty's whole theory of anti-submarine warfare had been based on the use of Asdic detection equipment and depth-charges for attack. By these means it was felt that seaborne trade could be adequately protected. The Germans, however, had developed new tactics which completely reversed this confidence. In the Atlantic, the U-boats organised themselves into groups (wolf-packs) for attack on convoys instead of by single craft, while another refinement was the surface attack by night when a U-boat was virtually immune from Asdic detection. The problem was only overcome when all escort vessels could be fitted with radar sets. In the meantime, since the MA/SBs could only operate at night because of their vulnerability to air attack, they were of little use for the purpose intended. Accordingly, the 22 craft completed by 1940 were converted into MGBs, armed with two pairs of .303inch Lewis machine-guns and two twin Vickers Mark V .5inch machine-guns in a power-operated turret. This High/Low Angle weapon had a range of 500 yards and fired belted armour-piercing tracer ammunition at 700 rounds per minute. The turret was hydraulically driven by a pump located in the engine-room and was controlled by a gunner seated in the turret. However, because of a severe shortage of the heavier weapon, the first of these craft did not become operational until early 1941.

Meanwhile, there was feverish activity to establish MTB bases along the southern and eastern coasts of Britain to receive the new flotillas being formed. In addition to two flotillas at Felixstowe, where the depot ship was HMS *Beehive*, others were in operation at Portsmouth (HMS *Hornet*), Harwich (HMS *Badger*) and Dover (HMS *Wasp*) by June 1940, and further bases had been established at Fort William, Portland and Fowey by the end of the year.

In Germany, too, this was a period of rapid expansion. With the occupation of Western Europe the E-boats had an ample number of bases available from which to make sorties against British convoys, as the Admiralty had feared. In July, the 1st and 2nd E-boat Flotillas were ordered to Boulogne, which became their main base for a while. A 3rd Flotilla was formed at Kiel, with Kapitänleutnant Friedrich Kemnade as commanding officer, and by the end of the year further bases had been established at Cherbourg, Le Havre, Ijmuiden, Ostend and Rotterdam, from where all three flotillas operated at different times.

Soon after the move to Boulogne, the harbour was attacked by British fighter-bombers – part of the RAF's offensive against the forces being assembled for the projected invasion of Britain – and several of the boats were damaged. In view of this, it was considered too dangerous to bring the depot ships to such advance bases. The boats had to be covered by tarpaulins as camouflage and moved their moorings several times a day, but in such conditions and without the depot ships, the problem arose of how repairs could be carried out. This was an essential part of operations, not only because of the damage that the boats might sustain while fighting but because the older craft especially were showing signs of stress and fatigue. Rust and engine corrosion were of particular concern. It was then that the idea originated of constructing bomb-proof concrete bunkers in which the boats could shelter and where repairs and maintenance could be carried out in safety. Such bunkers eventually became a feature of all the main E-boat bases in the North Sea.

The latter part of 1940 was primarily a time when both sides were preparing for the real battle that was to come. Although, on 8 September, the MTBs made their first successful torpedo attack when two boats from Felixstowe – *MTB.15* (Lt J.A. Eardley-Wilmot) and *MTB.17* (Lt R.I. Faulkner) – sank a German ammunition ship and damaged a cargo vessel off Ostend, the honours were clearly with the Germans. Following the first E-boat sortie across to the east coast on the night of 19/20 June, when the British freighter *Roseburn* was sunk off Dungeness, further successes were achieved until, by the end of the year, the three operational flotillas were able to claim the sinking of three destroyers, one mine destructor vessel, three trawlers and 23 merchant ships, the latter totalling 48,000 gross tons. Five E-boats were lost, three from mines, one through collision, and one sunk by destroyers of Nore Command on the night of 19/20 October. Because of the limited number of boats available, the damage they caused was little more than a nuisance value against the British convoy traffic off the east and south coasts. But with many more new boats preparing to come into service, the threat was unmistakeable. Not least was the capability the E-boats showed for laying mines.

GROWING THREAT TO COASTAL CONVOYS

The Germans were fully aware of the vital importance to Britain of her coastal convoys. Although as much traffic as possible was diverted to the west coast, the ports of the Clyde, Mersey and Bristol Channel were already congested with shipping from overseas, especially after the diversion of all Atlantic convoys to the north of Ireland and the closure of the ports along the English Channel to ocean-going traffic. At any particular time there was likely to be 100,000 tons or more of shipping assembled off the Firth of Forth, awaiting convoy down the east coast to Southend from where the vessels would then make their way into the Port of London. The number of ships in convoy often totalled around sixty, including some non-official camp followers, and strung out as they were in one or two columns along twenty miles of swept channel, the task of convoy control and discipline was not easy. By mid-1940, the U-boat offensive had been largely contained by the laying of mine barriers and regular air patrols by Coastal Command. These defences were sufficient to keep most U-boats away from coastal waters, and in any event there were fewer available since one-third of the German U-boat fleet at that time had been sunk and new craft had not yet come into service to take their place.

However, as in the case of the E-boats, German occupation of the entire North Sea coastline of Europe had given their short-range dive-bombers bases from which to launch hit-and-run attacks on coastal shipping. The slower aircraft of Coastal Command were unable to intercept the enemy and Fighter Command which was responsible for the air protection of coastal convoys, was engaged in its own life and death struggle in the Battle of Britain and did not have sufficient aircraft to provide the standing air patrols wanted by the Navy. Fighters were sent up whenever a German attack developed, but the German bombers had often completed their raid and departed before an interception could be made. Few of the merchant ships at that time were armed with anti-aircraft guns, and in any case their crews often lacked the necessary training and were as likely to fire at friendly aircraft as those of the enemy. This situation was not helped by the Navy's insistence that any unidentified aircraft approaching within 1,500 yards of a ship should be fired on, a ruling that was regarded as dangerous and irresponsible by the RAF. In July the Germans stepped up their bombing of coastal shipping, and for the first time losses from air attack off the east coast were higher than those caused by mines.

Meanwhile, attention was being focussed on that other area off Britain's coast, the English Channel, which was to remain the scene of fierce attack and counter attack throughout the war. Although the ports had been closed to ocean-going traffic as a result of the fall of France which gave the Germans coastal bases for their bombers and light craft such as E-boats, it was only through these ports that supplies could be brought for despatch throughout Southern England. Coal in particular, some 40,000 tons a week, had to be supplied in this way. Through-convoys of coasting vessels called CW and CE convoys were started between the Thames and the Bristol Channel, an extremely hazardous undertaking but there was no alternative. Losses rose alarmingly, from air attack by day and E-boat torpedo attack by night. One reason for the German success at this time was the establishment of a radio direction finding station on the rocky promontory of Cap Gris Nez which could detect the presence of shipping at sufficient distance to give air and naval forces ample time to make an interception. The observers and equipment were housed in a ramshackle old bus, taken there specifically for that purpose and effectively hiding what was going on from the eyes of RAF pilots who often flew low overhead.

The dangers of the Channel route are illustrated by the fate of one convoy in particular, CW8. On the afternoon of 25 July the 21 ships which had started out from Southend were passing westwards through the Strait of Dover at about 8 knots, escorted by a small group of RAF fighters. In spite of the continuous presence of the fighters, they were not sufficient to hold off an attack by a large force of enemy fighters and dive-bombers. Five ships were sunk by bombs and four more severely damaged. At this time, the MTBs of the newly formed 11th Flotilla at Dover were mostly employed for rescuing the crews of ships that had been bombed. Two of these MTBs were despatched to bring back survivors, making several trips to and fro in order to do so. Later in the afternoon, during a lull in the air attack, word came that six E-boats had been seen heading across the Channel, evidently intending to complete the destruction of the stricken convoy. The two MTBs, together with two destroyers, were ordered to intercept and set off at once for Cap Gris Nez. This could have been the occasion of the first engagement between E-boats and MTBs, but although the E-boats were sighted, they hung back behind the protection of the German shore batteries which had begun to open fire. The reason

Assembly point for an East Coast convoy, where a number of the merchant ships are fitted with barrage balloons and defensive armaments

was soon evident, when the Messerschmitt 109 fighters and Junker dive-bombers came over to renew their attack. Both destroyers were hit and badly damaged and the two MTBs were lucky to get away reasonably intact, although one had its steering shot away. After darkness had fallen, the E-boats which had come from the Boulogne base made their attack and sank three more ships by torpedo. Only eleven of the original convoy eventually passed Dungeness.

This loss compelled the Admiralty temporarily to stop the Channel convoys while additional defensive measures were devised. Fighter protection was increased and a number of small ships provided that could fly balloons, later formed into the Mobile Balloon Barrage Flotilla. The anti-aircraft gun defences on merchant ships were improved, together with the training of a special force of gunners known as the Channel Guard. The number of ships in a convoy was reduced to about a dozen while at the same time the escorts were increased, including the new 'Hunt' class destroyers. It became not unusual for a convoy to be led by minesweeping trawlers and closely escorted by as many as two destroyers, four anti-submarine trawlers, six MA/SBs or MLs, and surrounded by perhaps eight balloon vessels. Convoys sailed mostly at night, hugging the coast, and taking daytime shelter in various harbours along the route. By such means, although losses inevitably occurred sometimes, they were never again so serious. The enemy's attempts to close the English Channel to coastal traffic was defeated, although the amount of protection required was a heavy drain on Britain's air and naval resources.

For a while, after Channel convoys were resumed early in August, the Germans continued their attacks, but were soon dissuaded from pressing

them home too closely. The bombers in particular suffered heavily from the Spitfire and Hurricane escorts and the Luftwaffe turned its attention chiefly to inland targets. The E-boats meanwhile, now also operating from a new base at Cherbourg, had come to have a healthy respect for the British destroyers of the 'Hunt' and 'Jervis' classes being brought into service, considerably out-gunning them and even matching them for speed. After several E-boats had been damaged in encounters with destroyers the German Naval Command looked for alternative ways of attacking the vital coastal convoys. One was by shelling from long-range gun batteries constructed near Cape Gris Nez, remarkably ineffective as it turned out, although presenting the crews of the slow-steaming merchant ships with a new and nerve-racking ordeal. More successful was the introduction of attacks on the east coast shipping by torpedo-bombers of the German Navy's Air Arm. This was potentially dangerous and caused the Admiralty considerable anxiety, but in fact the Germany Navy was kept so short of aircraft, mainly due to jealousy on the part of the

Luftwaffe, that such operations were never fully developed.

The main German effort, therefore, was turned towards minelaying. This had proved highly successful earlier in 1940, although by mid-year the Royal Navy had learned to cope with the problems of the magnetic mine and losses from this cause had appreciably fallen. However, the Germans had developed yet another type of mine, the acoustic device which was detonated by the sound waves produced by the passage of a ship. At the same time, in the increasing battle of wits between mine-laying and mine-sweeping, magnetic mines were fitted with delay-devices, making it necessary to repeat every sweep, while explosive sweep-cutters often held up the clearance of moored minefields by destroying the sweeps. Since the German Navy had no fast minelayers, other vessels such as destroyers and especially E-boats were employed to lay them in British coastal waters. The latter were particularly well-suited for creeping close inshore, and here they were aided by the defensive minefield which the Royal Navy had laid offshore the east coast. Although highly effective in keeping out U-boats, markers had to be laid to show British ships where to leave and enter port through swept channels, and

these also indicated to the enemy where they should lay their own mines.

Night after night during the summer and latter half of 1940, the dozen or so E-boats available at that time made the run across the North Sea from favourably placed bases in Holland – Den Helder, the Hook and Ijmuiden – and swept channels across the Channel to the south coast from bases in France. Each boat usually carried twelve mines which were laid 1,000 metres apart. The dropping was done exactly to a prearranged timetable while two boats, not hampered by a cargo of mines and with all guns manned, guarded the flanks. Often these minelaying missions took the E-boats into sight of the shore, and on several occasions they penetrated the Thames estuary. Meanwhile, when the weather was suitable, up to 80 aircraft each night were also used to lay mines. As an illustration of the kind of difficulties created by this offensive, on one occasion during the night of 12-13 December more than 50 mines were laid in the Thames estuary between Southend and the Isle of Sheppey. Sweeping was begun immediately but failed to produce any result after four days. Then, when

'Hunt' class Escort Destroyer
Displacement: 907 tons
Dimensions: 280 ft x 29 ft x 7¾ ft
Engines: 2-shaft geared turbines, total 19,000 shp
Maximum speed: 26 knots
Armament: 2 x 2 4inch AA, 1 x 1 four-barrel 2pdr Pom-Pom, 1 x 1 single-barrel 2 pdr bow-chaser, 2 x 1 20mm AA
Crew: 146

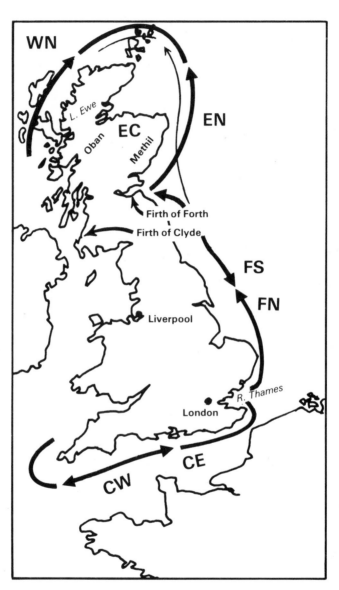

Coastal Convoy Routes

the danger seemed to be over, the mines suddenly started to explode. Seven ships were sunk in one day and losses continued for several weeks; the mines had been fitted with a mechanism to delay detonation for four-and-a-half days.

However, as had been the case with the magnetic mine, the Germans carelessly allowed a specimen of the acoustic type to fall into the Admiralty's hands by dropping several of them on land. A number of inexplicable explosions near ships during August and September had aroused suspicions that the enemy was using a new type of mine; now this was proved

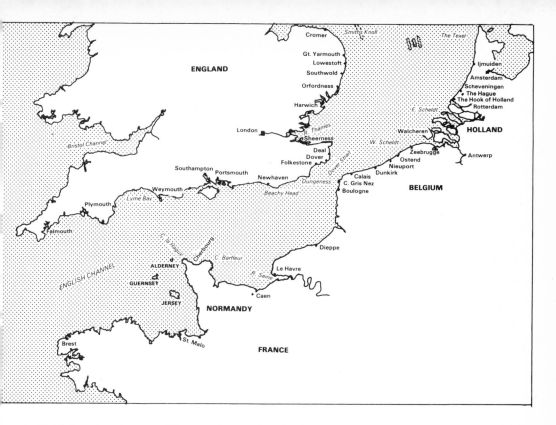

The English Channel and Southern North Sea

and British scientists could set about developing counter-measures. These were far from perfect to begin with and the sweepers themselves were sometimes damaged by the explosions of an acoustic mine ahead of them. It had been evident early in 1940 that the British minesweeping force of 400 vessels, originally thought to be adequate to deal with mines, was not sufficient to cope with the situation that had developed. Accordingly, by the end of the year, the force was increased to nearly 700 vessels, including converted trawlers, whale-catchers and drifters. Also, the first specially built fast minesweepers, ordered at the outbreak of war, were beginning to enter service. More than half of the total force was fitted to deal with the 'influence' type of mine.

Nore Command had the major task of keeping the swept channels off the east coast and as far down as the Thames estuary clear of mines. And it was not just the 4 million tons of coastal traffic leaving or entering British harbours during this period that was involved. Not all of the ocean-going ships that made the hazardous Atlantic crossing could be discharged on the west coast. A proportion had to be detached to steam in convoy round the north of Scotland and then combine with the regular flow of east coast shipping. These large ships bringing food and war materials from North America and other distant parts of the world presented the enemy with even more tempting targets. Minesweeping operations at this time were made more difficult by continual enemy bombing of the sweepers. This led to the decision in August to change from day- to night-minesweeping, with less risk to the vessels but presenting considerable navigational difficulties in an operation where precision was of the essence. Most of the normal navigational lights had been removed, but eventually special buoy lights were laid to mark the channels, shaded from overhead so as

HMS Valorous, *an old destroyer modified for East Coast escort duties, seen here taking up her station for another convoy. Note the twin 4inch AA gun forward; another was mounted aft, with two quadruple .5inch AA guns. These 'Wair' type destroyers supplemented the 'Hunt' class. The wartime censor has indicated that the pendant number and details of the topmast must be deleted*

not to be visible to passing aircraft. These proved a great success and enabled night minesweeping to be continued throughout the war. By such efforts, as well as the increasing use of the convoy system into which was brought about 90 per cent of coastal shipping, they succeeded in reducing losses due to mines from the peak of 22 ships – 86,000 tons – in June. Nevertheless, some 510,000 tons (201 ships) were lost to mines throughout 1940. About one-tenth of that total was attributable to minelaying by E-boats. More than half of the total lost was within the Nore Command area, showing the importance that the Germans attached to disrupting the east coast traffic.

COASTAL FORCES STRIKE BACK

Although the occupation of France and the Low Countries gave Germany an immense advantage in the establishment of coastal air and naval bases from which to harass British shipping, it did bring its problems as well. One of these was the need to supply the occupied ports along the European coastline and in particular the enemy's forces in western France. In this situation, there was a fundamental difference as compared with Britain. Britain had traditionally relied on its Merchant Navy not only to bring goods and materials from overseas but also to carry out much of the distribution required throughout the country, for which purpose its large coastal shipping fleet had been built up. Indeed there was little other alternative for road and rail services were not adequate to cope with the volumes involved. Europe on the other hand depended to a far greater extent on such services for inland distribution. Germany's mercantile fleet, for instance, was relatively small, and following her occupation of Europe, Germany expected to rely most on rail transport for the distribution of goods.

However, from the early stages of the war, rail transport and marshalling yards were a prime target for Allied bombers and later for attacks by the various Resistance movements. The resulting congestion and delays could be eased by the increased use of coastal shipping instead, since Germany now had available the merchant ships of the occupied countries. This did in fact become the German intention; equally, it was to prevent the build-up of such traffic that British efforts were directed at this time. In spite of the over-riding need to protect British coastal shipping, both the Nore and Dover Commands took whatever offensive action they could. The ideal craft for this purpose, as the Germans had discovered, were fast motor torpedo boats. A concerted effort was made to increase the number and quality of Coastal Forces craft, but it was not until mid-1941 that the results of this programme began to be felt. In the meantime, the few slow and ill-equipped craft that did exist, together wtih those destroyers that could be spared from defensive duties, were despatched on frequent sweeps off the coast of the Low Countries and on the French side of the Channel.

Targets were few and far between and even when faster and better armed boats became available, the MTBs never equalled the German E-boats in the numbers of ships sunk or damaged. This led some naval authorities to disparage the performance of the little ships, a view sometimes held to this day, while for the many crews who nightly made fruitless sorties without meeting the enemy there was only frustration and a nagging feeling that their efforts were a waste of time. What is often forgotten, however, is that the British intention was not so much to sink enemy merchant ships as to make it too difficult for a regular and unhindered flow of shipping to be developed. It was the threat that counted, with the additional benefit that those German armed ships and E-boats that had to be employed defensively as convoy escorts were thus prevented from taking the offensive against British shipping. MTBs did, of course, score some dramatic successes, but it was the threat that these underlined that was of the greatest value. It is on that seemingly negative objective, together with its success in combating E-boats and reducing their raids on British shipping, that the achievement of Coastal Forces in home waters throughout the war must be measured.

Although the need for such a policy became clear in the spring of 1940, the means of carrying it out was quite another matter. It was not only the lack of suitable craft but also the inadequacy of training and pre-war neglect in considering the kind of tactics that should be employed by MTBs. In this respect the German Navy had taken the initiative and although also hampered by a shortage of materials, the E-boat commanders had devised the basic methods of attack that were to be developed as the war progressed. The first MTB success on the night of 8 September 1940, described earlier, was followed by some others towards the end of that year, especially before the Germans learned to give their merchant ships better protection. In October, for instance, while providing cover for the monitor HMS *Erebus* which was to bombard the occupied coast from a position near the Kwinte Bank Buoy, three MTBs torpedoed and sank two enemy trawlers north of Calais, an operation notable for the fact that Lieutenant Dennis Jermain RN completed the destruction of one of the vessels by dropping a depth charge under it. He had previously studied such a possibility and it was a method of attack that was later developed wtih considerable success. Late in December a similar force of three MTBs, including Jermain and led by Lt R.A. Ellis RN in *MTB.32*, torpedoed and sank a large merchant ship anchored in the estuary outside Flushing.

But such achievements in the days before the boats were equipped with radar, were rare. Too often a wild dash into the night resulted in complete failure to make contact with the enemy. Or, if contact was made, the attack was mishandled. An example occured on 27 July 1941 when five MTBs of the 11th Flotilla stationed in Dover set out to attack a German destroyer in the Channel. Two of the boats narrowly escaped collision when crossing each other's bows at top speed, less than ten feet apart. The torpedoes were fired at too great a distance from the destroyer to have any chance of scoring a hit; one torpedo, in fact, barely missed hitting another MTB. And one of the craft fired at a British aircraft that happened to fly overhead at that moment, mistaking it for one of the enemy. It was a chapter of errors in which only luck prevented serious casualties. Small wonder that Coastal Forces' operations were often summed up officially as amateur and second rate, with attacks not pressed home hard enough.

Gradually, however, the crews learned from such mistakes. They found for instance that it was virtually useless to fire torpedoes at such ranges as 4,000 yards, which was not uncommon in the early days. The margin of error was too great, apart from the likelihood that the track of the torpedo would be spotted and evasive action taken. The problem was that an MTB speeding forward on main engines would be sighted at closer ranges and come under heavy fire, the least effect of which was for the points of aim to be blinded in the tracer. Quite early on it was found that a well-handled boat could creep up unseen to within several hundred yards of the enemy by using its silent auxiliary engine. Then, it was hoped, after the torpedoes had been fired and the MTB's presence revealed, the full speed of the main engines could be used to withdraw safely. From this method the MTBs went on to adopt the German tactics of waiting motionless in the expected path of an oncoming convoy. The problem here, especially on a dark night, was that a convoy could pass by unnoticed, even within a range of several hundred yards. The time spent lying in wait, and it could be some hours on occasion, was that much time wasted which could be used to cover the widest possible area in search of the enemy. Although searches on a shipping route off the enemy coast were usually carried out on quiet engines, there were times when, by starting up their main engines, the MTBs would reveal their presence to any enemy ships in the vicinity, which might then show their own positions by opening fire. The MTBs would then revert to a silent approach.

Once an enemy ship had been sighted and an approach made, preferably away from the moonlight, the decision had to be made as to the best angle from which to fire torpedoes. This called for considerable judgement by the Senior Officer or the commander of an individual boat. It was found for example that a target from behind had the advantage that the lookout in that direction was usually poorer, but the speed of the enemy and acuteness of the angle considerably reduced the chances of success. Firing from the quarter did in fact prove to be the worst position of all, not only because of the narrow target and the long time of flight which gave the enemy a chance to take avoiding action, as it required only a small alteration to course, but even if a torpedo did hit the angle was so fine that it could glance off without exploding. Slightly better was firing from the bow, since the deflection increased the hitting angle and the time of flight was shorter. In practice, the ideal firing position was found to be from an angle on the enemy's bow from where the torpedo could hit at 90 degrees to his track. With the whole length of the target exposed, the enemy had the greatest distance to turn if he sought to take evasive action. The actual angle of firing had to take a number of factors into account, of course, including the relative speeds of the torpedo and target and the distance the torpedo had to travel.

Among the other points learned at this time was discretion in the use of smoke so as not to provide more screen for the enemy than for oneself and hamper other craft that might be coming in to attack, and the vital need to report enemy sightings quickly in order that other boats could be despatched to the area. Even here there were drawbacks, however, since radio calls could warn an alert enemy of attack. Every action was different and had to be judged on its own account. At the speeds involved, in fighting at close quarters and in a constant stream of tracer and cannon-fire, MTB tactics called for the kind of cool, split-second decisions expected of a fighter pilot. With the difference that every time an MTB commander ordered a torpedo to be fired – one of only two or at the most four carried – he was spending several thousand pounds of the tax-payers' money. When attacking a small ship there was always the temptation to fire only one torpedo on the chance of meeting a bigger target later; however, the possibility of hitting any target was considerably increased by firing the torpedoes from both tubes at once. It was never an easy decision, and the number of torpedoes fired and missed during the early stages of the war did little to convince the Admiralty of the effectiveness of MTBs. Matters did improve, however; of the 1,328 torpedoes fired by MTBs throughout the war (out of a total of 7,720 by the Royal Navy as a whole, including naval aircraft), 318 were recorded as certain hits and 37 probable hits.

KEY TO GERMAN TYPE V ACOUSTIC TORPEDO CUTAWAY DIAGRAM

1	*Acoustic receiver*
2	*Thermal relay for safety range*
3	*Acoustic amplifier*
4	*Pick-up coils*
5	*Warhead*
6	*Solenoid locking pistol propellor*
7	*Coil operating pistol*
8	*Contact (inertia) pistol*
9	*Fusing relay*
10	*Compressed air reserve*
11	*Pistol amplifier*
12	*36-cell battery*
13	*Main switch (motor circuit)*
14	*Starting lever*
15	*Generator for homing gear supply*
16	*Charging plug*
17	*Pistol distributor box*
18	*Converter for pistol supply*
19	*G Switch*
20	*Motor*
21	*Depth control gear*
22	*Touching lever switch*
23	*Gyroscope*
24	*Discriminator switch*
25	*Contra-rotating gear*
26	*Tail unit & propellers*

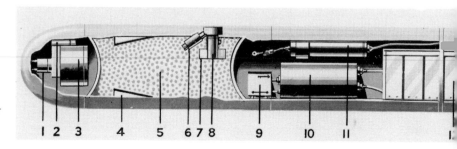

When cruising, MTBs usually maintained a V-formation. It was possible to keep station in line ahead but the wake of the boat ahead was often turbulent enough to make a craft uncontrollable. The only alternative was to increase the distance between each boat but this was difficult to judge correctly and produced a concertina effect as boats surged forward or fell back in their attempts to keep the right position. It was much simpler for a boat to keep station to the side of the one in front, just ahead of the wake in undisturbed water. In this way the distances apart were greatly reduced and there was no danger of overriding. However, the V-formation was not practicable in action where a sudden alteration in course meant that a boat might have to cut across the bows of the one astern. Also, boats were liable to be screened from the enemy by others in the same unit, an important factor in gunboat fighting, when as many guns as possible were needed to bear on a target. When an action was imminent, therefore, the boats either formed up astern or on a single line of bearing or were split up to operate individually, depending on the tactics decided upon by the Senior Officer. Should any boats be caught in the open sea during the hours of daylight and threatened with attack by enemy aircraft, they usually manoeuvred into a diamond formation which enabled the maximum concentration of anti-aircraft gun fire.

Early in 1941, while the MTBs stationed at Dover were involved in mostly unsuccessful skirmishes in the Channel, the first MGB flotillas were being formed from the converted MA/SB craft. The first was the 6th MGB Flotilla which early in March was sent to HMS *Beehive*, the Coastal Forces base at Felixstowe, under the command of Lt Peter Howes RN. At this time the E-boats had switched the brunt of their attack from the Channel to the east coast convoys. New flotillas were formed – the 4th under the command of Kapitänleutnant Niels Bätge and the 6th under Kapitänleutnant Albrecht Obermaier – and new boats were being brought into commission, partly to replace the older series. Minelaying operations were still carried out on occasion, but during the early months of 1941 the E-boats became much more aggressive with torpedo attacks

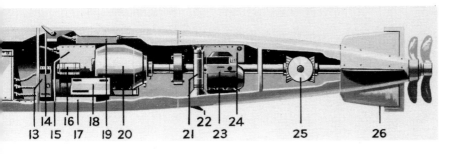

against convoys, exploiting the successes they had achieved in the Channel. Their normal route from Ijmuiden took them in a straight line across the Brown Ridge to Smith's Knoll, then southwards to patrol that part of the British convoy route lying off Norfolk and Suffolk, especially between Lowestoft and Great Yarmouth. So active did they become, in fact, that this passage was dubbed 'E-boat Alley'.

It was no joy-ride for the E-boat crews at this time, however. The winter had brought freezing temperatures that made it difficult to keep the boats operational and created other hazards, as illustrated by the experience of *S.103* (Leutnant zur See Künzel) at the end of January. Together with other boats of the flotilla, she left Ijmuiden with orders to attack the British convoy route near Brown Ridge Buoy, about half-way between the two coasts. The temperature was minus 16 degrees C and even at a reduced speed of 20 knots through the light swell, spray coming up over the bows froze immediately, covering the deck with a thick layer of frost. By listening on the VHF radio, the E-boats discovered that British destroyers were in the vicinity ahead of them. Suddenly, at about 2.30 am, Künzel sighted a four-funnel destroyer ahead of him, making about 25 knots. He increased to maximum speed and swung round to attack her broadside. But when he ordered the starboard torpedo to be fired, nothing happened. It appeared to be a dud.

The moon was shining brightly – rather too much so for the comfort of the E-boat crews – and *S.103* was sighted by the destroyer. A light flashed, ordering her to identify herself. Künzel replied by repeating the same

One of the smaller 82-ton E-boats, S.81, built by Lürssen in 1942 and showing the familiar built-in torpedo tubes with the armoured 'cupola' shaped bridge and 20mm AA guns forward and aft. The forward gun could be raised or lowered through a manhole. Although able to achieve a maximum 36 knots, the E-boats remained nearly horizontal in the water and did not lift their bows in the same manner as the planing craft of the British and American forces

morse-code letters – a trick also used by the MTBs when sighted by German ships – and turned away to make another attack. This time, the second torpedo fired, but passed harmlessly behind the destroyer's stern. Returning to base, Künzel found that the first torpedo which could not have failed to hit the destroyer was stuck fast in the tube by a layer of ice. It took a block and tackle to remove it – luckily after the torpedo rating had managed to unscrew the detonater. In order to avoid similar occurrences in future, the torpedo-tubes of E-boats were lined and sealed from the outside air by a coating of synthetic rubber which burst immediately a torpedo was ejected. This system bore fruit a month later, on the night of 25 February, when *S.30* (Oberleutnant Klaus Feldt) torpedoed and sank the destroyer *Exmoor*.

Some of the German claims for tonnage destroyed at this time were certainly exaggerated, not necessarily with intention on the part of the commanders, for as the British discoverd as well it was only too easy to mistake the report of a gun for a torpedo exploding, or to assume that even a resounding hit meant that the ship would sink. However, during the first four months of the year, E-boats did destroy 15 merchant ships totalling nearly 28,000 tons.

During the summer of 1941 E-boat operations in the North Sea declined when all the flotillas except the 4th were transferred to the Baltic to take part in the attack against the Soviet Union. Together with one new flotilla – the 5th under Kapitänleutnant Klug – they carried out minelaying patrols against Russian shipping off the Finnish coast. Some successes were achieved, notably the sinking of two surfaced submarines within the period of one week in June. One of these was destroyed by *S.35* (Leutnant Horst Weber) in an attack with depth charges and hand-grenades. The other was torpedoed by *S.60* commanded by Oberleutnant Siegfried Wuppermann. Overall, however, Baltic operations were not highly successful. There was little co-ordination between the Luftwaffe and the E-boat flotillas, so that such encounters as did occur depended more on luck than air reconnaissance. Also, the E-boats were very prone to mechanical breakdown. For most of this particular period in the Baltic, about one-third of the boats were in dock for repairs at any one time.

In the autumn of 1941 the E-boats were withdrawn from the Baltic, the 2nd and 5th Flotillas being transferred back to the west while the 1st went to the Black Sea and the 3rd was overhauled at Wilhelmshaven before being sent to the Mediterranean to support the Italian MAS boats in their operations from Sicily. During the summer, the 4th Flotilla had continued operations against British coastal traffic but without much success. However, with the return to the North Sea of two additional flotillas in October, increased operations brought better results, mainly by laying mines although torpedoes were used on occasion. One instance occurred on the night of 19 November when four E-boats from Ijmuiden (*S.41*, *S.53*, *S.104* and *S.105*) were sent to attack a convoy off Great Yarmouth. Three

HMS Watchman, *one of
the First World War
destroyers modified for escort
duties. Armament included
two 4inch guns, three
2-pounders, and two 20mm
AA guns. To the left of the
mast can be seen the special
'Headache' equipment for
monitoring radio
transmissions between
E-boats. The 'bowchaser'
2-pounder gun provided
close-range defence against
E-boats.*

ships were sunk, including the Fleet oiler *War Mehtar* of over 5,500 gross
tons. However, although it was little realised by either side at the time, the
operation that night marked a turning point in the war as British MGBs
fought back successfully for the first time against E-boats. It also brought
to public attention the name of the man who was to become the best
known MGB commander in the fight against E-boats, Robert Peverell
Hichens.

Hichens – or 'Hich' as he came to be known throughout Coastal Forces
– had joined the 6th MGB Flotilla as an RNVR lieutenant earlier that
year and during the summer had been operating from Felixstowe with the
converted MA/SBs. These were not powerful enough, however, to win a
decision over the E-boats and the few encounters that did occur had been
inconclusive. It was a frustrating period for the MGB crews, but it was
also a time of experimenting with new tactics. As a result of these experiences, it was Hichens who was partly responsible for pressing the Admiralty to hurry the order for the BPB boats specifically designed as gunboats. As an interim measure he managed to get the ex-MA/SB boats
equipped with heavier armament, either a 2-pounder Pom-pom, which
could fire at 98 rounds a minute with an effective range of 3,500 yards, or a
20mm Oerlikon cannon which became available in mid-1941 after plans
of this Swiss design were obtained and a factory for its manufacture had
been established at Ruislip in North London. This light rapid-firing gun
eventually replaced the .5inch machine-gun on all Coastal Forces craft,
and with it Hichens showed that even the unsuitable early MGBs could be
used effectively against E-boats. In August he took over as Senior Officer
of the 6th Flotilla, now a Lieutenant-Commander, and on the evening of

19 November three of the boats were lying in Felixstowe harbour at short notice: *MGB.64* with Hichens in command as overall leader, *MGB.67* under Lt L.G.R. 'Boffin' Campbell RNVR, and *MGB.63* commanded by Lt G.E. 'George' Bailey RNVR.

These nicknames, as well as that of 'Hich' stood for more than a simple spirit of comradeship. They were the call-signs by which individual boats were known so that they could be quickly identified over the R/T. The Germans employed the same technique, and this, in fact, was their undoing. For along the east coast, the Royal Navy had established a line of wireless listening stations, manned by WRENs, who night after night sat with earphones on, intent on picking up the radio messages being communicated between the E-boats. Eventually such call-signs as 'Rudi' and 'Bruno' and 'Karl' became almost as well-known to Coastal Forces as those of their own commanders. Such was the proclivity of the German crews for talking over the R/T that the British listening operation became known as 'Headache'. However, it had a very serious purpose, especially when introduced also in patrolling destroyers. Although 'Headache' could not provide an exact location of E-boats it did give warning of their presence when they crossed the North Sea on a raid and sometimes even an idea of the area they were making for. In this way, MGBs and destroyers could be sent out to try to intercept them. The Germans were surprisingly slow in realising just how they were giving away their presence, especially since they had their own listening operation (the B-service as it was called).

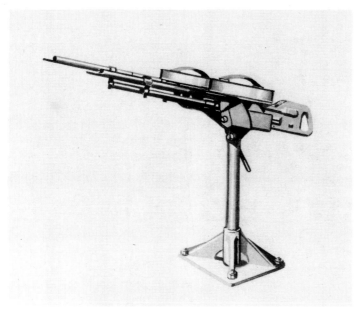

TWIN .303 VICKERS MACHINE GUN

It was by means of the 'Headache' system that Hichens was first given
warning that the four E-boats were heading towards the east coast convoy
route. He had little chance of intercepting them before they made their
attack, but from previous experience decided to cross the North Sea and
lie in wait for them off the Hook of Holland for their return. It was an ideal
night for small boats, with a flat calm sea and a high moon. Slowly, the
unit formed into line ahead and headed past the harbour boom. Once at
sea Hichens signalled full speed ahead, but almost immediately Bailey's
boat broke down with engine trouble. The fault could not be corrected so
she had to be left behind. A short while later mechanical trouble reduced
the speed of Hitchens' own boat to only 18 knots. With only one boat
capable of full speed and knowing the enemy were out in force, there
would have been ample reason to return to base. In any case it was no
longer possible to reach the Hook in time to intercept the returning
E-boats. But Hichens decided to go on and position himself instead at a
point some 20 miles to seaward of the area in which the E-boats were
operating on the convoy route, in direct line with the Dutch coast.

The two boats reached this position at 0200 on the morning of 20
November, cut engines and lay in wait for any sound of the returning
E-boats. Reports of their activities were still coming in, including news of
the three cargo ships they had sunk, so it meant a long wait. It was not
until 0445 that the faint murmur of engines was heard from the west. The
moon had set by now, and with a mist rising over the sea visibility was
reduced to little more than 200 yards. The chances of small boats meeting
in such conditions seemed very remote. Hichens started up, took a guess
at the enemy's course, and headed south-east in hope of intercepting
them. Every so often he stopped to listen. Sure enough, the sound was
growing much louder. Then suddenly, he caught sight of a blue light
winking quite close to port. The faint outline of a hull loomed out of the
mist. Although certain it was an E-boat, Hichens had to identify before
attacking. The reply to the challenge he flashed was indecisive. In fact, by
a remarkable chance, the two MGBs had come across the rendezvous
point where all the E-boats that had been operating in the area that night
were due to meet before setting course in a group for home. Hichens'
signal was assumed to come from another E-boat. As the MGBs moved
slowly forwards, they saw five E-boats ahead of them, moving slowly in
circles as they waited for the rest of their force.

Without hesitation, Hitchens ordered an attack at full speed. The two
MGBs surged in amongst the enemy, firing at a mere 50 yards range.
Before the Germans knew what was happening one was engaged to
starboard, another to port, and one which was moving slowly across
Hichens' bows was given a burst of fire from the forward guns at less than
20 yards. The E-boats' return fire was erratic, most of it passing harm-
lessly overhead, but at that range something had to hit and one burst put
Hichens' main gun out of action. By now the E-boats had somewhat

recovered from their surprise and were scattering in all directions. The speed of the MGBs was not sufficient to keep up with them. Deciding that the enemy's general disengaging course was likely to be south-east, towards the Dutch coast, Hichens headed in that direction, followed by Campbell. Suddenly, an E-boat showed up to starboard taking a parallel course. It was at that point Hichens found his starboard guns did not work, either jamming or having been knocked out. He had nothing with which to engage the E-boat except a stripped hand-controlled .303inch Lewis machine-gun. As he wrote later: 'The sense of frustration that I experienced at this moment is one of the liveliest and most vivid memories of my life. After a year's search for the elusive E-boat, to have one ranging nearer and nearer alongside at point-blank range, to be unable to fire anything at her except a rifle bullet, was utterly exasperating.' Not only that, but at any moment he expected a hail of 20mm cannon fire from the enemy boat, which at that distance could hardly fail to hit.

Then Campbell came roaring up in the other MGB with all guns firing. The E-boat swung hard to starboard, firing wildly, and in a moment was out of sight. Reduced to 18 knots, if they were to keep together, the MGBs had no chance of catching her. They kept on their south-easterly course but when they stopped after a while to listen, there was no sound of the enemy. The sheer closeness of the range in which the action had been fought had undoubtedly caused considerable damage to the E-boats. But without heavier armament, it seemed the MGBs had not been able to make it decisive. On the other hand, a quick examination showed that they themselves had been incredibly lucky. There were no serious casualties, and although Hichens' boat was slightly damaged, Campbell's was virtually unscathed.

Hichens was on the point of ordering a return to base when his coxswain reported a faint sound to the south-west. The two MGBs headed in that direction. Dawn was beginning to show in the eastern sky, dispelling the mist, and it would not be long before they were caught in that most vulnerable of all situations for motor torpedo boats – alone in the open sea during daylight, prey to any marauding enemy aircraft. Suddenly they saw ahead of them the long, white hull of a stationary E-boat, lying low in the water. There was no sign of life on her, and after a few moments of suspense and suspicion that it might be a trap, the enemy craft was found to be abandoned. She had been badly damaged in the action and left in a sinking condition after her crew had been taken off in another E-boat. It had been the sound of that departing boat that Hichens' coxswain had heard. In fact, although the MGB crews did not know it at the time, the damaged boat (*S.41*) had been holed earlier in a collision with another E-boat and both craft were in tow by their consorts when the British attacked. The other was taken safely back to Holland but *S.41* suffered so much additional damage from gunfire that she had been abandoned.

Every effort was made by the MGB crews to keep *S.41* afloat, for a

further important reason that the Admiralty was extremely anxious to have a close look at one of the German boats that were causing such destruction to coastal convoys. (As it happened, detailed plans and specifications of the Lürssen craft had been published in a British journal before the war but it was not until 1942 that this fact was noted by an alert officer looking through back issues.) But the seacocks had been opened and the engine-room flooded. As the water level rose, *S.41* began to settle by the stern. Everything possible was transferred to the MGBs and as the E-boat began to wallow in the water, Hichens reluctantly gave the order for her to be abandoned. The MGBs pulled away and stood off at about 50 yards to watch the end. The bow lifted slowly until, for several seconds, the boat hung vertically in the air. Then she slid quickly into the water and disappeared from view. A ragged cheer went up, but it was not enthusiastic. The crews felt something of the sadness experienced by all seamen at the sight of any ship going down.

The MGBs returned home to a triumphant welcome, flying the Nazi flag beneath the White Ensign. They had achieved their first success against E-boats, increased by later reports from a group of RAF fighters which had come across three E-boats limping home, obviously badly damaged. Two out-gunned MGBs, one of them not capable of more than 18 knots, had taken on and beaten five faster and larger E-boats. From this and later experiences the crews of Coastal Forces formed the idea that

The East Coast of Britain including the Thames Estuary

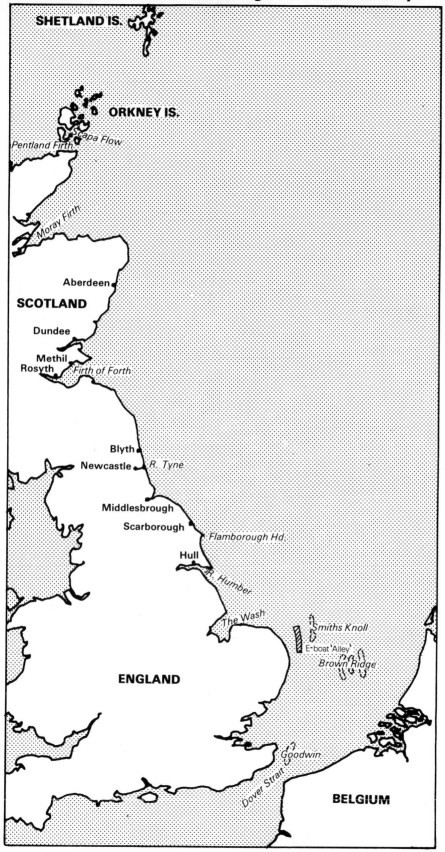

the Germans were afraid to engage them in battle, although possessing better and more heavily-armed boats. It was true that the Germans usually preferred flight to combat if attacked by MGBs, but this was due not so much to a lack of bravery or seamanship as the fact that they were under orders to avoid combat wherever possible. The E-boats were too valuable as weapons of attack against cargo ships and also too few in number to risk losing any in battles with MGBs. This set the pattern for the rest of the war, with the MGBs desperately trying to make contact with E-boats as they dashed across the North Sea in their hit-and-run attacks on coastal shipping. Only when the E-boats were used as escorts for German convoys did they show aggression against MGBs when the British craft made similar raids against the enemy-held coast.

Lt-Cdr Hichens went on to serve with distinction, not only as a flotilla leader but as the originator of most of the tactical theory that came to be used in motor gunboat warfare. He was awarded the DSO twice and the DSC three times before being killed in action in the early hours of 13 April 1943 by a final burst of enemy fire after a minor engagement had been broken off. He had been offered senior postings ashore, but preferred to remain in action with the fast boats he loved so much, and of which he wrote: 'I think one of the most lovely sights I have ever seen is a gunboat unit at speed in moonlight, with the white pluming wakes, the cascading bow waves, the thick black outlines of the guns darkly silhouetted, the figures of the gunners motionless at their positions as though carved out of black rock, all against the beautiful setting of the moon-path on the water.'

NEW BOATS

By 1942 new boats were being brought into service on both the British and German sides, with improvements in equipment and design as a result of earlier experiences in battle. Within Britain's Coastal Forces a distinction came to be made between short boats of under 100 feet and long boats of over 100 feet, applying to MTBs as well as to MGBs. Towards the end of 1941 supplies of the Packard engine began arriving from the United States and these were used to power virtually all the British craft, as they also powered the American PT-boats.

Vosper's second series of MTB, brought into service in 1942, was 72½ feet overall, 47 tons, powered by three Packard engines giving 4,050 hp and a top speed of 40 knots, armed with one twin .5inch and two twin .303inch machine-guns (later exchanged for one 20mm and then a 6-pounder was also added), two 21inch torpedoes, and carried a crew of 12 which was later increased to 13. Although there had been pressure from those serving in Coastal Forces for the very noisy main engines to be fitted with silencers, so that a quiet approach to the enemy could be made, this was not done until 1943; the 1942 boats were fitted instead with two Ford V8s in addition to their main engines which could be clutched to the outer shafts to drive the boat quietly at about 6 knots. It took time to change from these to the main engines and gave crews some hair-raising moments when they had to get away quickly from an action at top speed, usually while under fire. A third and last Vosper series came into service in 1944 with a slight increase in length to 73 feet, and carrying four 18inch torpedoes and armed with one twin 20mm, one twin .5inch, and two twin .303inch machine-guns.

In addition to the Vosper boats which provided the bulk of Coastal Force MTBs, 20 Thornycroft craft were taken over from other navies, 32 boats were built by J.S. White but powered by Sterling engines, and 38 American boats were acquired under Lend/Lease (29 Elcos, five Higgins, and four US Navy experimental craft). These saw most of the offensive action in home waters and the Mediterranean until the longer boats began to come into operation in 1942 and gradually took over the main role. Within this class of short boats there were also, of course, the MA/SBs and British Power Boat MGBs already described.

The first long boats to come into operation in 1941 were the Fairmile 'C' MGBs, and a need was soon felt for a long MTB which could operate further afield in heavier weather and carry more powerful armament. At the same time operations with small craft had shown that MGBs often missed opportunities by not carrying torpedoes. There was a requirement in fact for a combined MTB/MGB. Accordingly, the Fairmile 'D' was developed and began to come into service in 1942. Although short boats continued to be built, these 'Dog-boats' as they were called, bore the brunt of operations during the later stages of the war. Over 220 were built during 1942-44, of hard-chine, prefabricated double-skin diagonal mahogany construction, 115 feet overall, and powered by four Packard super-charged engines of 1,250 hp each. As combined MTB/MGBs they displaced 105 tons and had a top speed of 29 knots; as MTBs or MGBs only their weights were reduced to 95 and 90 tons respectively and speeds increased to 31 knots. This was due, of course, to the different forms of armament and the number of crew required which varied from 14 for the single-purpose craft to 30 for the dual purpose. As MGBs they first carried one 2-pounder, or twin 20mm, two twin .5inch and two twin .303inch machine-guns, two depth charges and one Holman illuminant projector; the MTBs carried the same armament plus two 21inch torpedoes. Eventually, the combined MTB/MGBs carried a formidable armament of two 6-pounders, one twin 20mm, two twin .5inch and two twin .303inch

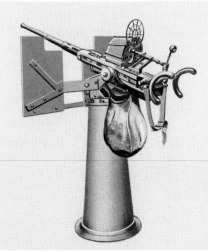

20mm OERLIKON CANNON ON DECK
MOUNTING

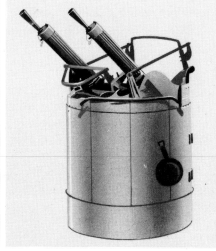

BRITISH 0.5in TWIN BROWNING MACHINE
GUNS IN DECK TURRET

machine-guns, and four 18inch torpedoes. They were the most heavily-armed boats of their kind in the world but they paid the penalty in considerably reduced speeds, and their large size, while providing better seaworthiness, made it more difficult for them to close an enemy unseen.

There were four further developments in long boats of the combined MTB/MGB type before the end of the war, all showing the tendency which had been apparent from the earliest days of gunboats in the previous century for navies to want to build bigger craft once they had found a successful design. This was especially the case with the Denny-built Steam Gun-Boats (SGBs), the first of which came into service in mid-1942. They were the largest of the Coastal Force craft, 145½ feet overall and displacing 165 tons, and armed with torpedoes as well as guns. Initially not too much speed was sacrificed, the two geared turbines of 8,000 hp giving up to 35 knots. But early operations revealed their steam machinery to be highly vulnerable to machine-gun fire and extensive modifications had to be carried out to fit armour plate. At the same time, armament was increased to include one 3inch gun, two 6-pounders and three twin 20mm cannon, as well as the two 21inch torpedoes. This in turn meant a larger crew of 34 and an eventual increase in displacement to 260 tons, reducing the maximum speed to 30 knots. Although the SGBs were certainly among the most beautiful boats ever commissioned in the Royal Navy, their size made them an easy target and they did not have the necessary speed to avoid action. All in all they were not a great success, and only seven were actually built of the 60 originally planned.

Also in 1942, eight Camper & Nicholson craft originally intended for the Turkish Navy were taken over by the Royal Navy; three were completed as MGBs, the others being used as mercantile blockade runners. Finally in 1943 came two experimental boats which were too late, however, to be developed before the end of the war. Vosper's built a 100-foot craft of 75 tons, powered by four Packard engines giving 35 knots and armed with one 6-pounder, two twin 20mm, two twin .303in machine-guns, and two 18inch torpedoes. And Fairmile produced one 'F' Type craft which, with four Bristol engines totalling 7,000 hp and giving a top speed of 36 knots, was one of the most powerful petrol-engined boats ever built.

Meanwhile, the British Power Boat short MGBs described earlier also came into service in mid-1942, the first of them going fittingly to Hichens' flotilla. From a modest beginning of only 18 MTBs and six MA/SBs at the start of the war, Coastal Forces had now been built into a formidable little-ship navy in home waters of 183 motor launches (shared more or less equally between all commands), 90 motor gun-boats (Nore 45, Dover 20, Portsmouth 15 and training 10), 70 motor torpedo boats (Nore 24, Portsmouth 16, Plymouth 8, Orkneys and Shetlands 8, Dover 7 and training 7), and six steam gun-boats based at Portsmouth. A further 80 MLs and 21 MTBs were based abroad, mostly in the Mediterranean.

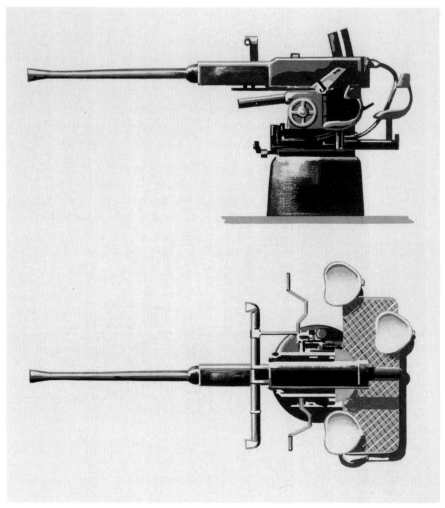

37mm AA GUN ON AFTER DECK

On the German side by 1942, two main types of Schnellboot were being constructed, one displacing 100 tons and 34.9 metres overall and a newer, smaller design of 82 tons and 32.8 metres. The latter was powered by three 1,600 hp diesel engines instead of the standard 2,000 hp engines and this was partly responsible for reducing its maximum speed to 36 knots, to the displeasure of the crews. There was another reason, however; operations had revealed a need to increase the fighting strength of E-boats, especially against MGBs when these began to arrive. The number of 20mm guns was increased to five, each with a protective shield, and eight 7.92mm machine-guns were also added. The overall result was an increase in the number of crew to 30. Later, the 20mm cannon in the stern was replaced by a 37mm AA or a 40mm Bofors gun.

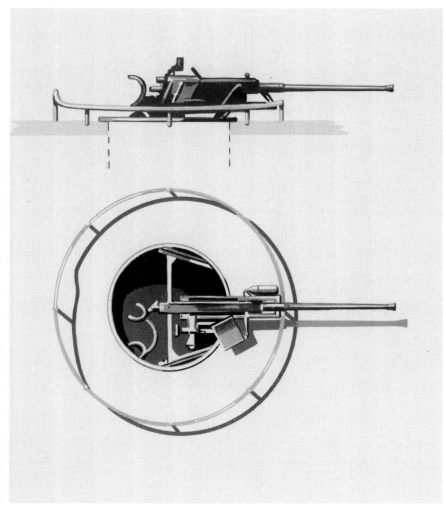

20mm AA CANNON IN FORWARD DECK WELL

Also, the need for armoured bridges became apparent after early skirmishes in the North Sea. To begin with, this was achieved by bolting armour plates to the existing structure, but in 1942 an entirely new armoured 'cupola' bridge was fitted. The additional weight resulting from all these developments had a further effect in reducing the previous maximum speeds of 40 knots, but some compensation was achieved by fitting the engines with super-chargers. By 1943, the three engines were giving a total of 7,500 bhp and a top speed of 42 knots in spite of the heavier armament.

The most powerful E-boat of all was the series beginning with *S.208*, brought into operation at the end of 1944. This displaced 105 tons and was powered by three 3,000 bhp diesels giving a maximum of 45 knots. Four

Overleaf: A surrendered German E-boat ties up alongside a Fairmile 'D' in Felixstowe harbour at the end of the war. The 37mm AA gun on the after deck was added to the larger types from 1944 onwards, and the rails on either side carried spare torpedoes or mines which were released from the stern

torpedoes were carried, together with the addition of a 37mm gun for use against air attack. An even bigger craft of 150 tons was designed but never built; it was intended to carry six torpedoes, two 40mm guns, and fitted with super-chargers to give each of the three engines 3,500 hp and a maximum speed of 46 knots.

Experiments were also carried out with much smaller craft. These were intended to be carried on board cruisers during their roving activities round the world against merchant shipping and lowered into the water when a suitable target presented itself. The prototype LS (light fast boat) was built in 1941 by the Dornier Works at Friedrichshaven on Lake Constance. It was only 13.4 metres overall but carried a crew of five and was armed with two 45cm (18inch) torpedoes, two 20mm guns and two machine-guns. Although powered by only two 850 hp engines it had a speed of 40 knots in calm waters, primarily due to the use of steel-reinforced light alloy for construction. This prototype was taken on board the auxiliary cruiser *Michel* into the Indian Ocean in 1942, but experience showed that the torpedoes were too small to cause much damage, even when they hit, which was not often owing to the craft's lack of sea-worthiness. Only very few of these boats were built. Even less successful was a slightly larger craft of 16 metres intended for use on the Russian lakes. They were so badly constructed, continually springing leaks, that the commander shipped them back to Germany as being totally unsuitable and a danger to their crews.

Although by 1942 about 25 Schnellboot hulls a month were being constructed, mostly by the Lürssen company, the maximum monthly delivery of engines was only a dozen, sufficient for only four boats. This was largely due to the decision to fit Daimler engines and none other while priority was given to the manufacture of such engines for other purposes. Indeed, after the bombing by British aircraft of the one factory turning out Daimler marine engines in 1944, there was a period when no engines at all were being produced. Delays in delivery remained a problem throughout the war, but nevertheless a total of 244 Schnellbooten were eventually brought into service. In addition, some 325 R-boats (Räuimbooten) were built, similar to the British MLs and used for minelaying, minesweeping, and coastal convoy protection.

In the United States, which entered the war on 7 December 1941 with the Japanese attack on Pearl Harbor, the decision had already been taken to standardise on two types of PT-boat, the Elco 80-footer and the Higgins 78-footer (of which 320 and 205 respectively were eventually built during the war). Both were designed for top speeds of at least 40 knots with a full load and a cruising range of 500 miles. While following a similar basic design, each had its distinctive below-deck layout. The Elco boat was slightly faster but the Higgins was more manoeuvrable. In terms of armament the first boats carried four torpedoes – 18inch to begin with and then 21inch – and two twin .5inch machine-guns. Then a 20mm cannon was added and an automatic 37mm mounted in the bow became standard in 1943, later replaced by two 40mm Bofors guns. Towards the end of the war experiments were made with 75mm guns, 4.5inch barrage rocket projectors, and 5inch spin-stabilised rockets. The increase in weight of gun-armament without a reduction in speed was made possible by the use of lighter torpedoes. The original Mark VIIIs carried by the first boats were manufactured to a 1920s design, heavy and slow and given to erratic runs, especially at shallow depth settings, and had to be launched through tubes to avoid upsetting the gyro. The tubes alone added to the weight. But with the introduction of the Mark XIII torpedo many of these drawbacks were avoided. It was not only faster (45 knots), more powerful and more reliable, but its non-tumbling gyro made it possible for it to be launched from simple racks on each side of the boat instead of through heavy tubes.

At the same time that new boats were being brought into service, changes were also taking place in organisation on both sides of the narrow seas. In Britain during the early days of 1940, although MTB bases were being established along the south and east coasts, Coastal Forces as a separate entity did not exist. Flotillas came under the authority of the different naval commands who used them as they saw fit. But rapid expansion made it necessary to form a separate organisation to coordinate the training of crews and the construction and manning of all the craft. The base at Fort William was reorganised for this purpose, under the

Opposite:
One of the original eight craft built for the Turkish Navy by Camper and Nicholson in 1942 but taken over by the Admiralty, this one was completed as an MGB while five became blockade runners, bringing machine tools and ball bearings from Sweden. The three MGBs (502, 503 and 509) were armed with a 2-pounder Pom-Pom in power turret forward, a twin .5inch machine-gun in power turrets on either side of the bridge, a twin 20mm Oerlikon in power turret amidships, a 6-pounder hand operated aft, and two twin .303inch machine-guns. This series displaced 95 tons and were powered by three Davey Paxman diesels of 1,000 hp each which gave a maximum speed of 28 knots, although super-charged Packards were fitted to MGB 509 to increase speed to 31 knots. When the blockade runners were no longer required at the end of 1944, they reverted to their original MGB numbers (504 – 508) and armament. In 1945 the surviving boats were rearmed and had 1500 added to their pennant numbers

5645

During the last year of the war, Camper and Nicholson built a series of powerful and heavily armed combined MTB/MGBs. These were based on a 1942 order for the Turkish Navy but taken over by the Admiralty and used as MGBs and blockade runners. The later series were designed with an increased beam and a spray strake since the first were found to be wet forward. Dimensions were length overall 117 ft, beam 22 ft 2½ ins, draught 4 ft 4 ins, and they displaced 115 tons. Three supercharged Packards gave a maximum speed of 31 knots and an endurance of 2,000 miles at 11 knots. Crew consisted of 3 officers and 27 men, while armament comprised a 6-pounder power turret forward, a 20mm Oerlikon on either side of the bridge and a twin 20mm amidships, another 6-pounder power turret aft, and four 18in torpedo tubes.

command of Lt-Cdr A.E.P. Welman. Then, in November 1940, Rear-Admiral Piers K. Kekewich was appointed Rear-Admiral Coastal Forces and the term came into being for the first time. But although Kekewich and his staff were responsible for personnel and technical development, operational control remained with the individual commands. Working first from Fort William, then Portland, and finally in September 1941 moving to a secret headquarters in London (a converted block of flats in the Finchley Road), Kekewich met with continual frustration in dealing with individual Commanders-in-Chief who were reluctant to give up any of their autonomy, and from Admiralty departments who hesitated to encroach on the established preserves of those commanders. It was not until 1943 that overall responsibility for Coastal Forces was brought under a separate department within the Admiralty.

On the German side, too, the early days were marked by a lack of organisation. At the start of the war, E-boats came under the Torpedo-boat command (with Konteradmiral Bütow as 'Führer der Torpedoboote'). This command was replaced by the Destroyer Command in November 1940, only to be restored again a month later. In April 1942 the torpedo-boat flotillas were again taken over by the Destroyer Command, and in the same re-organisation, the E-boats were established as an independent command, with Kommodore Rudolf Petersen as 'Führer der Schnellboote'.

IN THE
BALANCE

In spite of the threat from bombing, mines and torpedo attack, the east coast convoys had to continue. Indeed, they increased as a larger proportion of ocean-going traffic was diverted to the west coast of Scotland to join convoys passing northwards round the British Isles (WN convoys) and then combining with the FS convoy route along the east coast to the Port of London. In order to speed up the flow of shipping, fast convoys were introduced from Southend back to the west coast of Scotland (EC convoys).

The submarine threat had largely been contained by the laying of defensive minefields, and in any case the major German U-boat effort was now being waged in the Atlantic. But the coastal convoys were still vulnerable to attack by aircraft and E-boats, as well as from mines laid by both. The greatest danger in 1941 had been from the enemy's air assault, in which for one period sinkings by bombers averaged fifty-two ships a month of about 150,000 tons. When day-time fighter patrols increased, under RAF Fighter Command's new responsibility for convoy protection, the Luftwaffe switched to night attack, able to strike wherever it chose along the convoy route. Increased supplies of anti-aircraft guns and balloons on the ships themselves helped to make the enemy cautious of low-level approaches but the situation was still critical.

Towards the end of 1941, however, there was a decrease in enemy air activity, bringing a welcome reduction in shipping losses. This was partly due to great improvements in the defences. The escort ships were more experienced and now being fitted with radar, assisting the shore radar stations in giving warning of attack. An efficient system of co-ordination existed between the various services; no less than four commands, for instance, were involved in defending the Thames estuary – the Navy's Nore Command, the RAF's Fighter and Balloon Commands, and the Army's Anti-Aircraft Command. Forts had been constructed and sunk in the approaches to the Thames and equipped with heavy anti-aircraf batteries. However, the main reason for the reduction in German air raid: was Hitler's decision to invade Russia and the consequent diversion of the Luftwaffe's main strength to the Russian front. Knowing how vital Bri tain's merchant convoys were to her survival, it is a chilling thought to wonder what might have happened had Hitler not made that fatefu decision. As Captain S.W. Roskill wrote in his official *History of the War a Sea*, 'if Hitler, instead of attacking Russia, had concentrated the ful weight of his air power against our commercial ports, our docks and dockyards, our unloading and storage facilities, our coastal shipping and river estuaries, and had he kept the might of the Luftwaffe so directed fo months on end if need be, could this country have survived?'

Sporadic air attacks still continued, of course, usually at night by low-flying fighter bombers such as the Focke-Wulf 190 and Mes serschmitt 109 which could often approach unseen under the rada screen. Meanwhile, an even greater danger came from the E-boats shoul dering some of the minelaying operations previously carried out by air craft but also attacking with their torpedoes when conditions were suit able. At the beginning of 1942 there were three E-boat flotillas of 12 boats each operating against the east and south coasts of England, the 2nd, 4th and 5th, joined some months later by the 6th which had been based in northern Norway. A similar number of R-boats were used primarily fo minelaying. Following the tactics that had proved so successful in U-boa warfare, the Germans switched the emphasis of their attack abruptly from one area to another, hoping to catch the defence unawares. Thus for the first six months of the year, the E-boats were most active in the North Sea operating from Ijmuiden and the Hook to begin with and then from Ostend when the nights grew shorter, which almost halved the passage so that they did not risk being caught out in the open in daylight during the return journey. Then came a sudden shift to the Dover Strait and English Channel, operating from bases on the French coast. This was followed by a brief spell of activity in the Western Channel by two flotillas working from Cherbourg and the Channel Islands. Finally, the E-boats returned to the North Sea for the latter part of the year.

During the winter of 1941/42 the E-boats had things very much their own way. They were out every night when the weather was suitable, one favourite tactic being to lie on the far side of a lighted buoy until the convoy approached, then pick off the big ships in the lead and race fo home. It was in such a way that *S.104* (Oberleutnant Ullrich Roeder) on the night of 14 March torpedoed and sank the destroyer *Vortigern*. There were inevitably some losses, of course, and the E-boats came to have a healthy respect for the fast escort destroyers that were entering service. On that same day, *S.111* was sunk in action with *Guillemot* while *S.53* was lost after hitting a mine off Dover. For the most part, however, the E-boats avoided action with British convoys, concentrating instead on laying mines. In the first six months of 1942 alone, they laid 260 mines off the east coast which were largely responsible for the destruction of more than thirty Allied merchant ships totalling some 100,000 tons, as well as the destroyers *Vimiera* and *Whitshed*, and damage to the destroyers *Cotswold* and *Quorn*.

So confident were the E-boats at the start of the year that they broke their earlier rule and were often still at sea during the hours of daylight. Until that time, attacks on them by RAF fighters had been somewhat haphazard, usually confined to those occasions when they happened to sight the boats while on other missions. But in January, fighters of No 12 Group, sometimes joined by Coastal Command Beaufighters, began a series of specific operations against E-boats returning to base in mid-morning. The craft proved to be elusive targets and difficult to hit from a fast plane; in spite of some 90 attacks during the first two months of the year, no E-boats were sunk. However, these sorties eventually compelled the Germans to limit their operations to the hours of darkness, reducing the time available for minelaying and convoy hunting, and was one reason for the move to Ostend. This in turn put a larger burden of coping with them on the MGBs.

In spite of the rapid build-up of Coastal Forces – by the spring of that year there were operating within Nore Command six flotillas of MGBs, two of MTBs and eight of MLs (each flotilla consisting of eight boats at full strength) – it was still proving very difficult to intercept the E-boats. A plan was evolved for regular night patrols by MGBs and MLs operating from Felixstowe, Great Yarmouth and Lowestoft, stationed along a line some miles to seaward of the east coast convoy route from where it was hoped they could attack approaching E-boats. They were fed with a steady stream of information resulting from visual sightings and VHF eavesdropping by destroyers as well as shore stations. Plots were now helped by the network of coastal radar stations that was being established. But too often, the enemy managed to slip through and it was nearly four months before the MGBs were able to repeat Hichens' earlier success.

It was on the afternoon of 14 March that three fast Elco boats of the 7th MGB Flotilla from Lowestoft left harbour to take up an all-night patrol off E-boat Alley along with other gunboats and motor launches. The Senior Officer was Lt J.B.R. Horne in *MGB.88*, accompanied by *MGB.87* (Lt S.B. Bennett) and *MGB.91* (Sub-Lt P.A.R. Thompson of the Royal Canadian Navy). In spite of the disposition in the North Sea that night, a large force of E-boats managed to get through to attack the convoy route – and it was actually one of these boats that sank the destroyer *Vortigern* in the early hours of 15 March. Having been unable to prevent the E-boats breaking through, Lt Horne was ordered to take his boats across the sea to Ijmuiden to intercept them on their return. For hours they patrolled close to shore without sighting the enemy, then just before sunrise they came across an E-boat heading for home at top speed, serenely confident of safety in her own waters. The MGBs opened to full throttle and roared into the attack, forcing the E-boat to swerve off course, then followed alongside, shooting with everything they had. The Elco boats managed to keep up with every twist and turn made by the enemy, in spite of her 40 knots, and soon pieces of her hull and deck were flying in all directions. Such was the force of the attack that some of the German crew jumped overboard in panic. Others ran onto the deck with hands raised – and thus Coastal Forces received their first surrender of an E-boat.

Lt Horne hoped to bring the prize home, although she was badly damaged and low in the water. While two MGBs circled round to pick up survivors, a boarding party was sent to try to get the E-boat working again. Just as the boarders were reporting success, four more E-boats were sighted to the east, converging on the MGBs at full speed. Reluctantly, the E-boat had to be left, flying the White Ensign which had been exchanged for the Nazi flag. Now it was the turn of the MGBs to be chased, coming under heavy fire from the E-boats and very short of ammunition themselves. Suddenly *MGB.91* began to lose speed, one of her clutches broken. Seeing this, the other two boats laid a protective smoke-screen which helped to keep the E-boats off but also caused the British boats to lose contact. After searching in vain for the missing boat, there was nothing for the two undamaged boats to do but return home. Meanwhile, as the smoke cleared, *MGB.91* found herself with two E-boats on either side, coming in for the kill. With only two pans of ammunition left and unable to make more than 20 knots, it seemed that she must now be sunk or captured, an ironic turning of the tables. Lt Thompson prepared the confidential books for destruction and ordered one of his crew to break open the petrol tanks and set them alight. And then suddenly, he found himself engulfed again – only it was not smoke this time but thick fog. He turned away to avoid an E-boat which was dead across his bows, then set a westward course. By the time the gunboat emerged from the fog some while later, there was no sign of her pursuers. *MGB.91* eventually limped back to base with six of her crew of 13 wounded, two of them badly, and also one of the two German prisoners.

It was as a result of this action and others like it that the MGBs began to come to terms with the E-boats. Not every action ended with a decisive success and most of the night patrols failed even to make contact with the enemy. The North Sea was too vast an area for the little ships to cover adequately, and until the British boats came to be fitted with radar towards the end of 1942, it was only too easy for the opposing forces to pass within a few hundred yards of one another without realising it. The various buoys which marked both the British and German convoy routes were used by both sides as rendezvous points, and on more than one occasion on dark nights, E-boats and MGBs found to their consternation that they were moored practically alongside one another, each assuming the other to be friendly craft. Another factor that marked those engagements that did take place, especially before the boats on both sides were equipped with heavier armament, was the amount of punishment the little craft could take and still remain afloat. Each side claimed sinkings in good faith and only after the war was it discovered how many boats had managed to limp back to base in spite of being waterlogged. The big difference was in the types of fuel used. The petrol-driven British boats were extremely vulnerable to being set on fire, a hazard less feared by the crews of the German boats with their less inflammable diesel fuel.

The increasing number of British boats coming into operation, apart from the growing skill of their crews, was sufficient to ensure a rapid rise in the number of actions being fought. In fact, 1942 saw a peak in such battles which was not reached again until the Allied landings in Normandy two years later. It was a year in which the battle for the narrow seas between the German offensive to dislocate Britain's coastal shipping and the British determination to prevent this hung in the balance.

In addition to the convoy defences provided by escort destroyers and MGBs and MLs against actual attack by E-boats, the main British aim at this time was to make minelaying too difficult and expensive for it to be profitable to the enemy. A major part in this was played by the mine-sweeping force, for which nearly 1,000 ships of various kinds had been commissioned – although from the beginning of the war until mid-1942, some 140 of these vessels had been sunk through one cause or another. More than half of this force was based in the Humber, covering E-boat Alley in particular. The ships were now fitted to deal with all the different types of mine laid by the enemy, including magnetics, acoustics, and various combinations of the two, and during the previous year they swept no less than 1,285 ground mines from the coastal routes. So effective were the defences, in fact, that in May the Germans suddenly switched their main attack to the Channel area, the 2nd and 5th Flotillas operating variously from Calais, Dunkirk and Boulogne with an additional large force of R-boats to carry out minelaying in the Straits.

Dover Command, however, was fully alert to the E-boat threat and apart from the MTB flotillas that had been formed to attack German convoys along the French coast (whose activities will be described later), it had three MGB Flotillas operating from Ramsgate, Dover and Folkestone. These included some of the new British Power Boat Company 71½-foot gunboats of the type that had recently re-equipped Hichens' flotilla, while another new Coastal Force craft that had also just come into operation was the Steam Gunboat. Commanders such as Lt Stewart Gould, one of the most daring officers in Coastal Forces who was killed in 1943 while leading an MTB Flotilla during the North African campaign, had already achieved success, not only in defending convoys from E-boat attack but in attacking German merchant ships as well, although without the benefit of torpedoes and armed only with light guns, they were usually only able to inflict damage. With the arrival of the German boats at bases only a few miles away, the summer months of 1942 in the Channel became the busiest period of all for Coastal Forces, which saw a continuous series of battles with often several on the same night.

Interception by patrolling MGBs, aided by accurate plotting by the shore radar stations, proved minelaying to be a highly hazardous operation for the German craft which tended to come off second-best against the British craft, faster now and more heavily armed. The short nights also favoured the defence. And so, at the end of June, the two E-boat flotillas were suddenly switched to a new area of operations, transferring to Cherbourg with the object of attacking British convoys in the Western Channel. The base at Cherbourg now included a fully equipped engineering workshop where engines could be overhauled within 34 hours.

Plymouth Command which was responsible for British defences in the area, had done much less than other naval commands to meet such a threat. There had been very little E-boat activity in the Western Channel before, and owing to the autonomy of the individual commands and the touchiness of the Commanders-in-Chief towards anyone seeming to encroach on that, little had been done to disseminate information generally on small-boat warfare. Nore Command had, of course, learned a great deal about such tactics as a result of constant E-boat activity and had now appointed a Coastal Forces operational executive (Cdr. J.L. Younghusband DSC) to study methods in greater detail. It had been suggested that his advice could be given to other commands, but this was rejected on the grounds that it might seem to interfere with local authority. Consequently, when seven E-boats of the 2nd Flotilla under Kapitänleutnant Klaus Feldt (*S.48, 50, 63, 67, 70, 104* and *109*) set out from Cherbourg on the evening of 7 July, they faced an open sea empty of patrolling MGBs or MTBs.

In V-formation, the seven E-boats headed across the eighty miles of sea towards Lyme Bay which was on the regular Allied convoy route. The Flotilla Commander led in *S.104,* followed on his starboard by *S.67,* commanded by a highly experienced officer, Kapitänleutnant Felix Zymalkowski, who was to be given command of his own flotilla during the following year. In the cramped space of *S.104*'s wheelhouse the helmsman stood in the middle with the VHF telegraphist to the left of him and the engine-room telegraphist to the right. Higher up on the bridge stood the flotilla commander and the boat's captain, scanning the horizon through night-glasses. At the back of the wheelhouse was a tiny table where the navigator pored over his charts, plotting the flotilla's way through the swept channels of the German minefields, while down a narrow passage behind him was the wireless room, a centre for constant activity during an operational sortie. Messages from the shore base or other boats were being transmitted through a speaking tube from the telegraphist to the commander.

Half-hidden in a manhole in the forward deck, which could be raised or lowered as the occasion demanded, two gunners manned the 20mm gun, crouching down to avoid the spray from either side of the bows. On the after deck was one of the 37mm Bofors guns which had recently been fitted to the *S.100* series in place of the usual 20mm gun. On either side of the armour-plated bridge were spare torpedoes which could be rolled into the tubes, giving a total of four in all, unless depth charges were carried instead. Both the armoured cupola and the spare torpedoes were also among the improvements made to that E-boat series.

After nearly three hours at a cruising speed of 27 knots a message from one of the boats reported 'shadows to the fore'. Feldt ordered all the boats to stop, then led them forward slowly and quietly on single engines. Gradually, shapes loomed out of the darkness – a long line of freighters under escort by armed trawlers. Acting under a pre-arranged plan, four of the E-boats spread out in line abreast, each seeking an individual target. Blithely unaware of any possibility of attack, the convoy proceeded slowly on its way to Portland. The E-boats edged forward, reducing the range to 750, 600, then 500 yards. At that distance it was almost impossible to miss. And still, incredibly, the E-boats had not been sighted. At the very last moment, Feldt signalled the order to attack. With a mighty roar, the main engines were started. The boats leaped forward and seconds later two torpedoes were fired from each one. Tracer-fire flashed from the trawlers, but by now the E-boats had turned away, using their full 40 knots to get out of range. Explosions rent the air, but in the smoke of the battle it was not possible to see exactly what had been hit. Then the remaining three E-boats came in to the attack while the others re-loaded their tubes. The convoy had scattered in all directions by this time and the task of finding them in the darkness had become much harder. There was now the ever-present danger of the E-boats firing at each other in mistake for the enemy. And Feldt could not be certain if the feared escort destroyers might not be in the vicinity. Reluctantly, he called off the attack and turned for home, knowing that his flotilla had achieved a substantial success. And so it had. Six ships had been sunk: one Dutch and three Norwegian freighters, the trawler *Manor*, and the British motor tanker *Pomelia*, totalling 12,356 tons.

News of this disaster came as a shock to the staff of Plymouth Command. They had learned the hard way that small fighting craft were not to be dismissed so lightly but could be extremely lethal when the conditions were right and when proper measures had not been taken against them. The convoys plying the Channel route were just as important as those on the east coast, including as they did a proportion of ocean-going ships from the Atlantic convoys which left the main force in the Western Approaches. After running the gauntlet of U-boats in deeper waters it was especially galling to be put at risk by mere motor boats and within sight of home shores. Something had to be done, and quickly. There was no time to establish MGB flotillas from scratch. Accordingly, therefore, Hichens' flotilla from Felixstowe, now renumbered the 8th after being re-equipped with BPB craft, was transferred to a new base at Dartmouth to combat the E-boats. He arrived on 14 July and on the very next night achieved his first success – not, ironically, against the E-boats but by sinking a German tanker off Alderney in a depth charge attack, coming across the enemy ship by accident after waiting fruitlessly all night for the targets he expected.

It was not until just over two weeks later, on the night of 2 August, that Hichens encountered the E-boats, now operating from St Peter Port in Guernsey in addition to Cherbourg. It was a decisive battle. Four MGBs, commanded by Lt R.A. 'Bussy' Carr, Lt 'Boffin' Campbell, Lt 'George' Duncan and Lt T.R. Ladner (the last two being Canadians), with Hichens on board Carr's boat, took on an equal force of E-boats just off Cherbourg and in a fierce twelve-minute action succeeded in destroying two of the enemy at virtually no cost to themselves, only leaving the scene when the German shore batteries opened fire.

Shortly after this encounter, and somewhat demoralised by the sudden appearance in these waters of 'Hich', for whom the Germans had come to have a healthy respect, the two E-boat flotillas returned to their French bases eastwards along the coast to resume operations in the narrow Channel. Hichens remained for another month at Dartmouth before his flotilla too returned to its normal base of operations on the east coast. The threat in the Western Channel had been contained, and preparation now began on forming MGB flotillas to be based permanently at Dartmouth, Plymouth and Portsmouth. At the same time, the fortuitous sinking of a tanker by Hichens had shown that the Western Channel could be a fruitful hunting ground for the British as well. As there was less danger from mines in the deeper waters there, destroyers could operate in combination with MTBs, as had originally been planned. A strong force of such craft was formed and carried out many successful sorties between Cherbourg and Ushant and among the Channel Islands.

Meanwhile, German E-boats and R-boats were making a desperate effort to lay a large quantity of mines in the Dover Strait, both offensively in the British convoy route and defensively to seaward of their own, to protect their supply ships from increasing incursions by British destroyers and MTBs. This operation was no less hazardous than before, and so the German naval staff decided on a new ruse. Their boats would set out before dark in the hope of completing the task of minelaying before the MGB night patrols were in position. This meant risking attack by RAF fighters, but evenings of poor visibility were to be chosen in order to reduce the chance of being spotted.

The first that Coastal Forces knew of this plan was on the evening of 16 August when, shortly after 2030 hours, the Dover radar station reported a large force of enemy craft leaving Calais on a north-westerly course at 15 knots. This was unusually early for such a sortie since, although the weather was overcast and reduced visibility to less than a mile, the sun was still up and would not set for more than another hour. Two of the smaller boats, *MGB.6* and *MGB.10* under the command of Lt G.D.K. Richards – had already set out from Ramsgate on patrol while three of the larger Fairmile 'C' boats – *MGBs.330, 331* and *609* under Lt D.C. Sidebottom – were just preparing to leave Dover. Both groups were ordered to converge in mid-Channel on the enemy force, which had now been identified as between 20 and 30 R-boats, putting the odds at around five-to-one. The action that followed was to become a classic in Coastal Forces' operations.

Soon after leaving harbour, the steering of Richards' craft, *MGB.10*, broke down when the rudder connections parted. Leading Motor Mechanic John Wibrin, one of the unsung heroes of the little ships who had to work in an incredibly cramped space to keep the engines going no matter what was happening up on top, crawled into the after compartment and found that he could hold it in place by hand. This he did, in the noise and heat of the small area under the exhaust pipes, throughout the following 70 minutes of the engagement – 'a feat requiring almost incredible endurance and devotion to duty', as stated in the citation awarding him the DSM. Meanwhile, the three MGBs from Dover were speeding in line ahead when, at 2125, they sighted six enemy boats which had parted company from the main force. Just as Sidebottom was about to attack, receiving no reply to his challenge, Richards' two MGBs appeared. In order that the two groups should not accidentally fire on each other, Sidebottom's slower boats moved to attack the rear while Richards' faster boats overhauled the enemy group to attack the leading boats.

The R-boats had not made any attempt to open fire, obviously mistaking the MGBs, because of their manoeuvres, for escorting E-boats. Sidebottom's three boats overhauled the enemy line to port, on a parallel course, and at a range of less than 100 yards opened fire with every gun on the last two craft. This fire was immediately returned by the enemy boats, whose gunners had been waiting with fingers on the trigger. With the distance continually closing neither side could miss. The wireless on Sidebottom's boat was hit immediately, so that he could not make the report 'enemy attacked' to base. Then both the 20mm and 2-pounder guns were knocked out, after firing only a few rounds. The following MGBs were also heavily hit. But the two enemy boats suffered even worse from the shells bursting over their hulls. With nearly all his guns out of action, Sidebottom was faced with a difficult decision. The action was too fierce for any signals to be passed between his boats, and if he turned away to disengage, the other two boats would take this as a signal to follow, in accordance with established tactics. They would lose the chance of finishing off the two enemy craft. If he stayed where he was, on the other hand, he was a sitting target for the enemy and would almost certainly be sunk. Therefore, he took the only alternative course and swung sharply to port to ram the last enemy boat. This enabled the other two MGBs to move forward to attack further enemy boats up the line.

Just before the impact, the enemy's after gun scored direct hits on *MGB.330*'s bridge, wounding everyone including Sidebottom. As the coxswain collapsed, the wheel spun free and the boat lurched away. It would have missed the enemy but Sidebottom, the only one on his feet, grabbed the wheel and brought her round again. Aided by the force of the enemy's wash, the MGB's bows ripped into the R-boat's port quarter. The impact was so great that members of both crews were thrown off balance, some of them being knocked unconscious. Locked together, both boats turned out of line, leaving the other craft to speed away from them. The MGB's engines were still running at high speed, keeping her bows forced into the side of the enemy, but the number of casualties made boarding impossible. Sidebottom ordered the engines stopped. The enemy boat gradually drew away into the gathering darkness, smoke billowing from her deck and water pouring into the gaping hole in her side. Shortly afterwards she sank, a fact confirmed later by survivors who were picked up and taken prisoner.

But *MGB.330* had also suffered badly. All the guns except the starboard twin .5inch were so damaged as to be useless. The steering and port engine were out of action, and fires had broken out in six places. Two members of the crew were dead, eight wounded, and two were suffering from carbon dioxide gas which filled the engine-room. In spite of the fumes, they managed to put out a fire that had started when the petrol tanks were punctured and restarted the engines. Other members of the crew rigged up the hand tiller and put out the other fires. One of the worst was under the bridge and its glow through a shell hole was attracting gunfire from other enemy boats. And so AB Victor Willingdale, one of the gunners who had been wounded with the rest of the Pom-Pom crew, lay in front of the hole to screen the glow until the flames could be put out. Eventually, the crippled boat was brought back to harbour.

Meanwhile, the other two Fairmiles had continued to engage the enemy at close quarters, severely damaging the last boat in line. But intensive return fire from the craft ahead hit *MGB.609*, killing four of the crew and wounding most of the others including her commander, Lt Alan McIlwraith. She kept going, with only the twin Oerlikon still working, until a shell hit the engine-room and with only one engine in operation, McIlwraith had to disengage. The third MGB carried on alone until her guns too were put out of action and her commander, Lt N.R. Weekes, and two other members of the crew were wounded. Both these boats also limped back to harbour.

During the few minutes in which this fierce action took place, Richards had taken his two MGBs to the head of the enemy line, engaging the leader first to port and then circling to attack to starboard, making use of their speed which was nearly twice that of the R-boats. Fire broke out on enemy craft and distress signals were fired. *MGB.10* was hit on the waterline and one engine put out of action, but neither she nor *MGB.6* had suffered any casualties. Most of the fire from the by now thoroughly rattled enemy passed harmlessly over the gunboats which, being smaller and faster than the Fairmile MGBs, were more difficult targets to hit. Ordering *MGB.6* to stand by, Richards took his boat alongside the stationary R-boat. Although the fire appeared to be out, smoke was still coming from her. Two of the MGB's crew, Sub-Lt Philip Lee and Leading Stoker Robert Mackenzie, jumped on board with the intention of overpowering the crew and making fast the tow ropes. They found half a dozen dead bodies lying on the deck, but the rest of the crew had abandoned the stricken craft. Suddenly there was a loud explosion amidships as the R-boat's ammunition store blew up. Flames swept through the craft and Lee and Mackenzie only just managed to jump back onto their own boat in time. The tow ropes which they had already secured had to be cut immediately to allow the MGB to pull away from the burning wreck before she sank. *MGB.6* in the meantime had picked up eight of the R-boat's survivors from the water, and later *MGB.10* rescued another seven.

When the events of that night were pieced together and the German survivors interrogated, it became apparent that the MGBs had not only sunk the two enemy boats but also had badly damaged three more, two of them to such an extent that they might well not have been able to return to base. In fact, one did so but the other had to be abandoned in a sinking condition. The whole operation had been highly successful, resulting in a long list of awards to the MGB crews.

Shortly after this, the E-boats returned to the North Sea which had in the past proved to be a more fruitful area of operations. But they found that the situation had greatly changed during the spring and summer months they had spent in the Channel. With more boats available, including the new and improved types, Coastal Forces had established permanent MGB and ML patrols some eight miles to seaward of the east coast shipping lanes. Radar was now being extended to detect and plot enemy boats up to 20 miles offshore, and the sets being fitted to Coastal Forces' craft themselves greatly assisted the task of interception. It was no longer a matter of trying to catch E-boats during their return passage to base; now the MGBs had a good chance of engaging them before they could attack the convoys. There were occasions when the E-boats did slip through undetected, showing the need for constant vigilance. On 7 October, boats of the 2nd and 4th Flotillas attacked a convoy off Cromer, sinking three cargo vessels and a motor launch. Shortly after the arrival of the 6th Flotilla from Norway to strengthen E-boat forces in the North Sea, three of its boats on 14 October torpedoed another two cargo ships off Cromer.

In November the 5th Flotilla was again switched temporarily to the

Western Channel and sank three cargo ships off Eddystone Light, while in the early hours of 3 December, *S.115* (Oberleutnant Joachim Klocke) sank the 'Hunt' class destroyer *Penylan*. Back in the North Sea, the biggest success of the period occurred on the night of 12 December when five E-boats of the 4th Flotilla slipped undetected through the patrol line and attacked convoy FN 889, sinking five freighters totalling over 7,000 tons. Throughout the whole of the year in western operations, E-boats sank by torpedo two destroyers, four trawlers, one motor launch, and 20 merchant ships. They laid some 1,900 mines which were largely responsible for the loss on the east coast of 21 ships of 43,000 tons.

These losses were by no means neglibile, but they have to be seen in the context of the enormous amount of traffic along the east coast. From the beginning of the war until mid-November 1942, no fewer than 63,350 ships had sailed in the FN, FS, and EC convoys, of which only 157 had been lost from all causes. The most serious losses in the early months had been among independently-routed ships, but now nearly all the ships made the voyage in well-escorted slow and fast convoys. With a reorganisation of coastal convoys towards the end of 1942, an average of 36 sailed each way between the Thames and the Forth on six days out of seven. Between the Thames and Portsmouth, convoys of about 18 ships sailed in each direction once every six days. On a new route between Plymouth and the Bristol Channel, PW and WP convoys of about 20 ships sailed every two days, with smaller convoys of some seven ships run at the same interval between Portsmouth and Plymouth.

With so much shipping available for the E-boats to attack, and comparing this with the actual losses, it was readily apparent by the end of 1942 that the balance had swung in favour of the British. Coastal Forces had achieved their primary task of combating the E-boats, gaining a measure of control over the narrow seas. There could be no let up, of course. The Germans tenaciously continued their E-boat operations in these waters, often against considerable odds, and slipping through to sink Allied vessels by torpedo or mine if ever the defences relaxed. Had they not been deprived by their own Naval Command of the numbers of craft they urgently requested, these losses would have been even greater. As it was, however, the main threat posed by the E-boats in 1941 and earlier in 1942 had largely been overcome. And with the defence gaining the upper hand, Coastal Forces could now turn more of its attention to the offensive, taking the battle to the enemy's own coast in attacks on German coastal convoys. With this change in the fortunes of war, the E-boats increasingly had to take on the task of protecting their own convoys, just as the British boats had done earlier.

COASTAL FORCES TAKE THE OFFENSIVE

During the period mid-1941 until early 1942, the Germans were successful in getting a substantial number of convoys and warships through the English Channel, usually at night by moving in short stages from one port to another, and taking full advantage of bad weather. The traffic was considerably less than on the British side – for example, between April and June 1941 some 29 merchant ships of over 1,000 tons and 11 destroyers were known to have made the passage – and this meant that considerable escort forces could be made available as well as the cover provided by aircraft and coastal guns.

The boats of Coastal Forces were primarily engaged at this time against German minelayers and E-boats, and even when attempts were made to take the war to the enemy coast, the MTBs found it difficult to locate targets. When they did so, it was even harder to penetrate the screening escorts to attack the larger ships. However, a few successes were achieved which, apart from their value in boosting morale, pointed the way for the future. The MTB and MGB flotillas based at Dover found that instead of operating independently, it was beneficial for both types of craft to work together. Thus the MGBs would take on enemy escorts, especially E-boats, and drive them away in a series of running battles, while the MTBs slipped through the defence screen to attack the ships being escorted. A noteworthy example of this technique occurred on the night of 3 November.

While two MGBs led by Stewart Gould (with Lt M. Fowke commanding the second boat) engaged the escorts of a convoy sailing through the Dover Strait, two MTBs commanded by Lt-Cdr Pumphrey (with Lt P.A. Berthon commanding the second) torpedoed and sank a 5,000-ton merchant ship and got away before their presence had even been detected. Gould's MGBs did sustain considerable damage and casualties, but not before they had shot up a trawler escort and severely damaged a German

'T' Class torpedo boat, equivalent to a small destroyer. The teamwork developed by Pumphrey and Gould had a great influence on the tactics later adopted more generally by Coastal Forces. It also showed the value of having one boat that could combine the dual role of gunboat and torpedo boat, and hastened the development of the larger Fairmile 'D' class boats.

Another technique tried out during this period also had a profound effect on later tactics, both offensive and defensive. This was the method of using MTBs or MGBs in conjunction with a destroyer which, through its more sophisticated radar and VHF devices, could locate enemy craft and vector the smaller boats towards them. This was not the original intention, however, when the first of these combined operations took place. Among the Coastal Force flotillas that had been formed at this time were those manned by Dutch, Norwegian, Free French and Polish crews (later in the war, American PT-boat flotillas were brought over to operate in the English Channel during the Normandy invasion). A Norwegian MTB flotilla was based at Scapa Flow and the decision was taken to carry out an attack off the Norwegian coast. The MTBs did not have sufficient range to make the two-way passage under their own power, and as an experiment, on 1 October, it was agreed that one would be towed across by a destroyer. The boat in question was *MTB.56*, commanded by Lt Per Danielsen, towed by the Norwegian destroyer *Draug*. Some thirty miles from the Norwegian coast, the MTB slipped away from the destroyer and quietly entered a fjord south of Bergen. The Germans had not expected such an attack and were sending a fully laden tanker northbound with only a light escort. Lt Danielsen torpedoed and sank the tanker, together with one of the escorts, and then sped away to rejoin the destroyer and be taken in tow once again for the return journey. Both got home safely without damage or casualties.

This attack and other Commando raids on the Norwegian coast convinced Hitler, wrongly as it happened, that Britain was about to invade Norway. It was for that reason he decided to bring three powerful warships back into German waters from their base at Brest, involving a spectacular run through the Dover Strait during the hours of daylight. The three ships were, of course, the battlecruisers *Scharnhorst* and *Gneisenau* and the heavy cruiser *Prinz Eugen*. They made the run on 12 February 1942, escorted by no less than ten torpedo boats and a large number of smaller escorts including E-boats, with 16 aircraft providing continuous air cover. Among the attempts made to prevent this convoy getting through was an attack by five MTBs from Dover, led by Pumphrey, but the escort screen was too concentrated for them to get through. Equally unsuccessful but more tragic was a later hopeless attack against overwhelming odds by six Swordfish of the Fleet Air Arm, led by Lt-Cdr E. Esmonde. All the planes were shot down, with only five survivors being picked up (Esmonde was posthumously awarded the Victoria Cross).

HMS Stayner, *one of the US destroyer escorts built in 1943 for the Royal Navy which was specially equipped for anti-E-boat work, including surface radar and a 2-pounder bowchaser*

Further attacks by aircraft and destroyers were also beaten off, and by the morning of 13 February the warships arrived safely in German waters. The fact that both the *Scharnhorst* and *Gneisenau* had been damaged by mines while off the Dutch coast could not disguise the German success in running the gauntlet through the Channel, almost within sight of the English shore. It was yet another example – although the most dramatic one to be sure – of a situation in which too many German ships were able to make the coastal voyage unscathed.

The United States made a considerable contribution to the escort and minesweeping forces of the Royal Navy, including the building of turbo-electric frigates (USN destroyer escorts). HMS Holmes, one of the 'Captain' class, was armed with a 2-pounder 'bowchaser' in addition to the normal three 3inch, and eight 20mm guns. She was fitted as a Coastal Forces control ship

*Twin 6pdr Gun Mounting
Mark I*

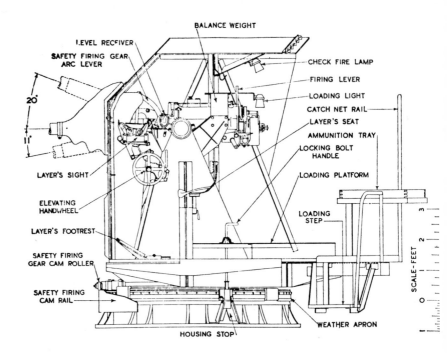

BALANCE WEIGHT

LEVEL RECEIVER

SAFETY FIRING GEAR
ARC LEVER

CHECK FIRE LAMP

FIRING LEVER

LOADING LIGHT

CATCH NET RAIL

LAYER'S SEAT

AMMUNITION TRAY

LOCKING BOLT
HANDLE

LOADING PLATFORM

20°

11°

LAYER'S SIGHT

ELEVATING
HANDWHEEL

LOADING
STEP

LAYER'S FOOTREST

SAFETY FIRING
GEAR CAM ROLLER

SAFETY FIRING
CAM RAIL

WEATHER APRON

HOUSING STOP

SCALE - FEET

LEFT SIDE ELEVATION

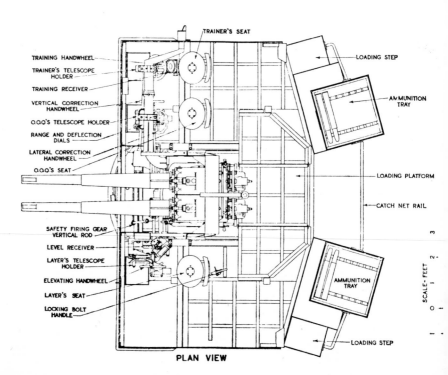

TRAINER'S SEAT

TRAINING HANDWHEEL

LOADING STEP

TRAINER'S TELESCOPE
HOLDER

TRAINING RECEIVER

AMMUNITION
TRAY

VERTICAL CORRECTION
HANDWHEEL

O.O.Q'S TELESCOPE HOLDER

RANGE AND DEFLECTION
DIALS

LATERAL CORRECTION
HANDWHEEL

O.O.Q'S SEAT

LOADING PLATFORM

CATCH NET RAIL

SAFETY FIRING GEAR
VERTICAL ROD

LEVEL RECEIVER

LAYER'S TELESCOPE
HOLDER

AMMUNITION
TRAY

ELEVATING HANDWHEEL

LAYER'S SEAT

LOCKING BOLT
HANDLE

SCALE - FEET

LOADING STEP

PLAN VIEW

During the following month another large ship, the disguised raider *Michel*, also made a successful run down-Channel, from Kiel to La Pallice, in spite of attacks by destroyers, MTBs and MGBs. By May, however, when a second disguised raider *Stier* also made the voyage from Rotterdam to the Gironde, the British forces had become more experienced. Although *Stier* got through undamaged, two escorting torpedo boats – *Iltis* and *Seadler* – were sunk by MTBs with heavy loss of life, for the loss of *MTB.220*, in which the Senior Officer Lt E.A.E. Cornish and most of his crew were killed. Taking also into account the increased efforts of RAF Coastal and Bomber Commands to disrupt the enemy's coastwise shipping, especially by minelaying, the summer of 1942 began to prove very hazardous for German convoys in the Dover Strait. It was for this reason that the Germans made a major effort to lay defensive minefields in mid-Channel to protect their shipping lanes, work that was mostly carried out by E- and R-boats with the results described in the previous chapter.

A major contribution in tipping the scales in favour of Britain was a rapid increase in the number of boats being commissioned in Coastal Forces, including the new designs. In mid-June, for instance, the 1st SGB Flotilla was formed at Portsmouth and within a few days undertook its first successful operation. This was on the evening of 18 June when three of the gunboats, under the command of the flotilla's Senior Officer Lt J.D. Ritchie, set out in company with the 'Hunt' class destroyer *Allbrighton* to intercept two German merchant ships which were known to have left Le Havre with an escort of E-boats. *SGB.7* commanded by Lt R.L. Barnet, succeeded in sinking a 3,000-ton merchant ship by torpedo in the Baie de la Seine, but was herself sunk by an E-boat; Lt Barnet and most of his crew were taken prisoner. The main reason for this loss was the SGB's lack of speed in withdrawing after the action, and as a consequence, no further craft of this type were ordered although the Admiralty had originally envisaged a force of 60. However, the remaining six continued to give excellent service in the Channel and later in operations from the Shetlands. What proved to be highly successful was for SGBs and destroyers to work together, the latter making up for the gunboats' vulnerability when up against E-boats. This kind of combined attack, in which the larger ship could give covering fire and illuminate the target for the smaller boat to make a torpedo attack, had been suggested at the beginning of the war when the Admiralty was considering how Coastal Forces could best be employed. But until 1942 there were not sufficient destroyers available, in view of pressing demands elsewhere, especially as convoy escorts in the Atlantic.

Command of the SGB Flotilla was later taken over by Lt-Cdr Peter Scott, MBE, DSC and Bar, son of Captain Scott of the Antarctic and a distinguished artist and ornithologist. It was he who created one of the most successful ship's camouflage schemes of the war, blending duck-egg blue, off-white and green to such effect that on one occasion two ships disguised in this way collided in mid-ocean before being aware of each other's presence. This camouflage was designed primarily for invisibility at night and broke away from the seemingly logical but entirely false notion which had previously been accepted that because the night is dark, dark colours should therefore be used. The Germans, with the grey-white colouring of their E-boats, were the first to find the opposite to be true; that if a ship was visible at all at night it was in the form of a dark shape against a moonlit sea, so the purpose of camouflage should be to paint her in lighter colours.

The first of the larger but slower Fairmile D-boats to see action was *MGB.601* (Lt A. Gotelee), which set out from Dover on the night of 20 July in company with two Fairmile 'C's to search for enemy patrols south of Boulogne. The force was led by Lt. H.P. Cobb, with Lt G.D.A. Price commanding the other boat. Gotelee's boat was not in fact armed with torpedoes on this occasion, which proved to be a drawback when they encountered a German convoy, a few miles north of Cap Gris Nez, comprising a merchant ship escorted by a number of armed trawlers and R-boats. The sea was too rough for small MTBs from Dover to reach the location in time, and so Cobb led his force in an attack with guns only, intending to drop a depth charge in front of the merchant ship if he could get close enough. The MGBs met a murderous fire from the escorts which set Cobb's boat ablaze and caused casualties in *MGB.601*. Several enemy vessels were also hit and burning, but then Cobb's boat blew up; a few survivors were taken prisoner, but Cobb was among those killed. As a result of the action, some modifications were made to all the other D-boats still being built and it was not until the end of the year that they came widely into use with the opening up of a new theatre of operations off the Norwegian coast.

By the autumn of 1942 it had become a major operation for the Germans to send a large merchant ship or warship through the Channel. On those occasions when it was tried, a single vessel might be escorted by a dozen or more E-boats or armed trawlers. These usually succeeded in getting their charge through unscathed when attacked by small units of British craft, as witness the previously described action. But it was another matter when an equally strong force could be despatched against such a convoy. This was the situation in the Western Channel where, following Hitchens' success earlier in the year, large numbers of destroyers, MTBs and MGBs had been based at Dartmouth, Plymouth and Portsmouth for the purpose of clearing those waters of enemy shipping.

Early in October, following their success in despatching the raiders *Michel* and *Stier* down-Channel, the Germans decided to try the same with the 4,000-ton armed merchant raider *Komet*. This was a new and important ship, fast and heavily armed. She had returned to Flushing at the end of 1941 after her first cruise, and now it was intended to take her round the coast in the Western Channel from where she could set out to attack the Atlantic convoys. The first stage of the voyage began at midnight on 7 October when the *Komet* left Flushing with a strong escort of minesweepers and torpedo boats. Early in the morning of the 8th, however, four of the minesweepers were themselves mined and the warship had to put into Dunkirk. She left four days later and coasted in stages to Boulogne and Le Havre, finally passing Cherbourg in the early hours of the 14th.

Meanwhile, the Admiralty had become aware of an important movement on the other side of the Channel. Five destroyers from Portsmouth, under Lt-Cdr J.C.A. Ingram in the *Cottesmore*, four more from Plymouth, and eight MTBs from Dartmouth were sent out against the convoy. Contact was made off Cap de la Hague by the first destroyer group, which set fire to the raider and two of her escorts. The second group of destroyers then arrived and engaged the other escorts, every one of which was damaged. *Komet* was still making 15 knots and in the smoke and confusion of the battle there was some danger of her getting away. However, the MTBs had arrived by then and one of them, *MTB-236* commanded by Sub Lt R.Q. Drayson, managed to slip unseen between the shore and the enemy ships. *MTB.236* crept ahead of the raider on silent engines, then at a range of only 500 yards delivered the *coup de grâce* with two torpedoes. The explosion as *Komet* blew up was heard on the English coast, some 60 miles away.

In the North Sea, also, Coastal Forces began to take the offensive as the arrival of both short and long MGBs enabled the MTBs to be used for the purpose originally intended, that of attacking enemy coastal shipping with torpedoes. Here again, as with the defensive measures devised against E-boats, tactics were gradually evolved after a period of trial and error. And just as the names of the individual Senior Officers of flotillas had emerged during particular periods of the war – Hichens' MGBs at Felixstowe and in the west country, the Pumphrey-Gould era at Dover – so a new name came to the fore as a pioneer of MTB operations in the North Sea. This was Lt Peter Gerald Charles Dickens, RN (great-grandson of the novelist, son of Admiral Sir Gerald Dickens, later promoted Lt-Cdr and including among his awards the DSO, MBE and DSC).

Earlier in the war, as a regular officer, Dickens had been first lieutenant of a 'Hunt' class destroyer on east coast escort duties. It was during that period that he came to appreciate fully the importance of coastal convoys and their vulnerability if coastal waters were not sufficiently guarded. It was a lesson to be sharply underlined when, on 20 April, his ship, the *Cotswold*, was severely damaged by hitting one of several mines laid by E-boats the night before. Ironically, the MGB which picked up some of the casualties from *Cotswold* was the one commanded by Robert Hichens. The two men met fleetingly for the first time; later they worked closely together as Senior Officers respectively of MTB and MGB flotillas based at Felixstowe.

Dickens accepted with enthusiasm his appointment as Senior Officer of the 21st MTB Flotilla which was based at various times at Portsmouth, Dartmouth and Lowestoft, before settling permanently at Felixstowe. His first attempts to take the war to the enemy's coast were not exactly glowing successes. This was generally the experience of the MTB flotillas at that time, acting under the vaguest of orders and with little by way of precedence to show them how to fight this unaccustomed form of warfare. The Admiralty's most urgent consideration was in protecting Britain's coastal shipping and little thought had been given to attacking that of the enemy. But as Dickens recently wrote in a book of his wartime experiences (*Night Action*, published by Peter Davies in 1974), important targets did exist, especially in the iron ore from Sweden which was vital to the German war economy and for which by far the best route was by sea to Rotterdam and thence by barge up the Rhine.

Left very much to his own devices, Dickens approached the problem from two main standpoints, firstly a scientific study of the technique of attack, in which he encouraged free-ranging discussion among his commanders, and secondly the need for discipline and training so that the tactics evolved could be carried out correctly. From the beginning, he drilled his crews in close-station manoeuvring at all speeds, so that each commander was instantly alert for signals and the slightest deviation by other boats. Even simple details were of vital importance – for instance, he insisted that commanders always carried plenty of handkerchiefs to wipe the spray from their night-glasses to keep them in good condition for viewing. As regards tactics, he saw the MTB's role as that of a hunter stalking a quarry, in which the best method of attack was not a blind, headlong rush forward with little time for aiming correctly at the enemy, and in any case warning him of an attack, but instead a deliberate, unhurried approach which gave an opportunity to manoeuvre into the best position for firing. Even if a torpedo missed, there was still the possibility of changing course to fire from another angle. Such tactics called for a cool determination and greater degree of courage than a quick hit-and-run to get it all over as rapidly as possible, but under Dickens' own inspiration they paid ample dividends in the end.

As with all the most resolute MTB commanders, Dickens believed in the importance of firing anything at the enemy, even small arms, although the damage they could cause was negligible. In his case, however, there was more involved than a spirit of aggression born of the desperate days when boats were sent out armed merely with .303inch Lewis machine-guns. In his analytical approach he saw that any kind of gunfire could disconcert the enemy gunners and make their own return fire more inaccurate than it might otherwise have been. However, guns were to be fired only if an MTB's presence had been detected. On one particular occasion, Dickens' methods probably saved the lives of himself and his crew. Before leaving on a night patrol the coxswain of another MTB which was in dock for repairs asked if he could come along in Dickens' boat. Dickens agreed, provided the man brought a gun along with him. During an engagement some while later, Dickens found himself in the highly dangerous situation of having all his guns knocked out, one engine broken down, and surrounded by E-boats which were closing in for the kill. Suddenly, from a position just under the bridge, a single Lewis gun opened fire. It was the coxswain who had come along for the ride, his presence forgotten by Dickens. As a result of the unexpected burst of fire, the enemy's aim was temporarily upset, their boats hesitated, and the MTB had time to get the broken engine going again and move away out of trouble.

Basing his tactics on creeping up on the enemy unobserved, to get as close as possible for a torpedo shot, Dickens also developed a system for his boats to split up in accordance with a pre-arranged plan if one was sighted. That boat would start firing and manoeuvring at high speed, not doing any particular damage but drawing the enemy's fire and attention, giving the other boats a chance to approach quietly from another direction. If they were seen, they in turn would make a lot of noise while the first slowed down and itself tried to make an unobserved attack. With this method in mind, it became apparent that MTBs and MGBs working together would make an ideal combination. This had already been inaugurated by the Dover-based flotillas, but Dickens and Hichens developed it to an art as a result of the painstaking training of their crews. It was the basis, in fact, of Dickens' first major success when, on the night of 10 September 1942, on board *MTB.234*, he led another (*MTB.230* commanded by Lt J.P. Perkins) supported by three MGBs (led by Lt E.D.W. Leaf) against an enemy convoy off the Frisian Island of Texel. It was a classic combined attack by the two types of craft that later became a regular technique in Coastal Forces. While the MGBs kept the enemy escorts busy the MTBs slipped in quietly at slow speed and torpedoed and sank an armed trawler and damaged another. Less than three weeks later, on 30 September, Dickens led a similar kind of attack on an iron ore convoy in the same area and sank both the merchant ship *Thule* and one of the escorting armed trawlers.

The end of 1942 saw Coastal Forces gaining the ascendancy over their rivals in the North Sea and English Channel and this might have been even more marked had it not been for the particularly bad winter of 1942/43. Rough seas severely restricted the operations of the smaller craft, such as the 72½-foot Vosper second series with which Dickens' flotilla was equipped. The time was not wasted, however. Improvements were made in the organisation of Coastal Forces on shore which went part of the way towards solving the problems that had hampered the work of Rear-Admiral Kekewich in his difficult and somewhat anomalous position. Early in 1943, Coastal Forces became the overall responsibility of two Admiralty departments, with Captain F.H.P. Maurice appointed Director of Coastal Forces Material (primarily concerned with the development and building of boats) and Captain D.M. Lees DSO appointed Deputy Director Operations Division (Coastal). A working-up base had already been established at Weymouth (HMS *Bee*) under Cdr R.F.B. Swinley, and not only were new crews being trained there but existing crews were seconded from operations during the winter lull to take part in the courses provided. Somewhat to their surprise, they found that they still had much to learn about gunnery, signals, torpedo drill and general tactics. All this reflected the greater degree of importance that the Admiralty had come to attach to Coastal Forces, a far cry from the early days when they were little understood and regarded very much as the poor relations of the Royal Navy. One of the most significant developments at this time, from the point of view of actual operations, was the appointment of Captain H.T. Armstrong, DSO and Bar, DSC and Bar, RN, as Captain Coastal Forces for the whole of Nore Command to co-ordinate and improve training and tactics.

Meanwhile, during those winter months Coastal Forces activities by no means ceased altogether. While the operations of the smaller craft were inevitably reduced, it was now that the larger D-boats proved their worth in being able to withstand heavier weather and with an ability to operate further afield because of their increased range. It was with this in mind that the Norwegian-manned 30th MTB Flotilla operating from the Shetlands was equipped with Fairmile 'D's and began a series of operations against enemy shipping in the fjords of the Norwegian coast. The new boats could now make the crossing there and back under their own power without having to be towed by destroyers as before. The flotilla was commanded by Lt-Cdr R.A. Tamber and achieved its first success in the early morning of 27 November 1942 when two boats managed to enter the Skjaergaard fjord unseen, in spite of a brilliant moon, and sank two 7,000-ton merchant ships by torpedo. The MTBs returned home unscathed, although they had to cope with a strong gale on the way back. Further successes followed, and the MTBs also took part in a number of Commando raids on enemy coastal installations. Later, the Norwegian flotilla was reinforced by a British one commanded by Lt-Cdr K. Gemmel DSO, DSC, and operations from the Shetlands continued until the last days of the war.

The Fairmile 'D's were also operating in greater numbers now from the east coast bases, where their increased range enabled them to hunt for enemy shipping round the Hook of Holland in places least expected by the Germans. It was Gemmel in fact, based at Great Yarmouth (HMS *Midge*) early in 1943 before being transferred to the Shetlands, who scored the first successes. On 9 March he led the flotilla against an enemy convoy off Terschelling and sank a 6,500-ton tanker together with two of her escorts; during the action, however, *MTB.622* commanded by Lt F.W. Carr was destroyed by gunfire from German destroyers. The sight of *MTB.622* sinking with all hands in a raging inferno was very much in the minds of Gemmel and his crews when the flotilla set off for the same area again three nights later. Another convoy was sighted almost at the same spot, three large merchant ships surrounded by smaller escorts. The MTBs fired their torpedoes at a longer range than was usual, nearly 3,000 yards, and hit two of the merchant ships. One broke in two and sank fast, the other caught fire first and then sank more slowly. The MTBs turned for home, the enemy being unaware of their presence from start to finish of the action.

A feature of this period of operations was an increasing degree of co-operation with other services concerned in coastal warfare, particularly with Fighter Command and Coastal Command in which short-range aircraft worked with destroyers and MTBs in attacking enemy convoys. In Nore Command, fighter-bombers of the Strike Wing of Coastal Command's No. 16 Group occasionally went on night patrols to locate such convoys, dropping flares to act as a guide for the MTBs. In Dover, too, new tactics were developed involving co-operation with Albacores of the Fleet Air Arm and heavy gun batteries on the Kent coast. On the same night as Gemmel's second success off the Dutch coast, 12 March, three of the Dover MTBs were lying at short notice in the harbour. The Senior Officer of the flotilla, Lt B.C. Ward DSC, was just going to bed at about one in the morning, thinking it too late for anything to happen that night, when news came that a heavily escorted German merchant ship had left Boulogne on one of the enemy's rare attempts to make a dash through the Strait. The three MTBs, *38* (Lt Mark Arnold-Foster DSC), *35* (Lt R. Saunders DSC, RANVR), and *24* (Lt V.F. Clarkson), put to sea at once, with Ward in *MTB.38*. The convoy was already being fired upon by the big guns at Dover, and as the three boats reached the interception point, they found that aircraft of the Fleet Air Arm were also going into the attack. In the light of the starshell bursting overhead and with the additional help of the enemy's tracer firing up at the planes, it was not difficult to sight the merchant ship. At that moment, a force of MGBs led by Lt G.D.K. Richards DSC arrived and engaged the escorting German patrol boats. Both Saunders and Arnold-Foster fired their torpedoes, the latter's hitting and sinking the merchant vessel.

Efforts such as these showed that there was still a place for the short boats, especially in waters nearer home. Even further afield, where the MTB/MGB D-boats were achieving a higher proportion of successes, the smaller Vospers could still make themselves felt if handled in the right way. This was certainly the case at Felixstowe where Dickens was now Senior Officer of the 21st and 11th MTB Flotillas (the latter commanded by Lt I.C. Trelawny DSC). One such operation took place in the early hours of 14 May when four MTBs led by Dickens torpedoed and sank two German minesweepers off the Hook of Holland.

Such was the pattern of MTB operations throughout 1943, with the exception that activities in the English Channel showed a marked decline in the summer and autumn as the Germans seldom dared to run a convoy through. Three flotillas of SGBs, 'D' Type MGBs, and 70-foot MTBs based at Newhaven did begin to operate in a new area off the Normandy coast, although the German radar-controlled gun batteries mounted high on the cliffs made this a particularly dangerous hunting-ground.

But what of the E-boats during all this time and their own offensive operations against British shipping?

STALEMATE

The two great Commando raids of 1942 – on St Nazaire in March and Dieppe in August – together with smaller operations against the Norwegian coast, in all of which Coastal Forces had played a vital role, proved beyond doubt the importance of controlling coastal waters even in a modern war. This might seem self-evident but it was a lesson that both sides had tended to neglect. In spite of the Germans' earlier superior strength, they had never been able to penetrate Britain's coastal waters to land on British soil – and it was not just a failure to gain complete control of the air that prevented Hitler's plan to invade in 1940. Now, it was clear that a major Allied assault on Germany's European fortress was only a matter of time. Command of the narrow seas would be a vital factor on both sides but Germany, with the long occupied coastline of Western Europe, was especially vulnerable.

Rather surprisingly, in view of the superiority in numbers of Britain's Coastal Forces over the German E-boats, the overall situation in small fighting boat operations in 1943 was one of stalemate. Although both sides made desperate attempts to attack the coastal convoys of the opposition, shipping losses as a result of torpedoes fired or mines laid by these craft were relatively very few. This was largely due to the introduction of radar systems on both sides, which gave warning of an impending attack, and better convoy escorting by destroyers and other heavily-armed ships which made it extremely difficult for small craft to penetrate the defensive screens. Paradoxically, however, both the MTBs and E-boats still served an important function. Because of MTB forays against German shipping of the kind described in the previous chapter, the E-boats were often forced into the defensive to act as escorts for their own convoys. This reduced the scope of their offensive activities against British shipping. On the other hand, they could still strike back when the opportunity arose, both in direct torpedo-attack and laying mines. Thus they succeeded in tying down a large British defence force which could well have been used elsewhere, especially destroyers in the Atlantic battles against U-boats. It was apparent that destroyers were the most effective weapons against E-boats, confirmed after the war when German records showed that the E-boat crews feared them much more than the MGBs whose guns were seldom heavy enough to deliver a knock-out blow. The fact that so many destroyers had to be retained in British home waters – 24 in Nore Command and 22 in Rosyth to escort the east coast convoys, and 4 in Portsmouth and 9 in Plymouth to escort the Channel convoys – showed how seriously the E-boat threat had to be taken. In such a situation, with neither the MTBs nor the E-boats succeeding very well in the purpose for which they were originally intended, it was equally true that if either side let up and relaxed its offensive or defensive operations, it would suffer a heavy penalty.

An example of destroyer action occurred on the night of 17-18 February when a group of E-boats of the 6th Flotilla set out to lay mines in the shipping lanes off Yarmouth. They were detected by shore radar and reported to the destroyers on patrol. Two of these, *Garth* and *Montrose*, intercepted the enemy boats and sank *S.71* by gunfire. Such engagements were by no means always one-sided, however, and the E-boat was still a weapon to be respected. When, on the night of 13/14 April, six boats of the 5th Flotilla encountered Convoy PW 323 off Lizard Head, they found the merchant ships escorted by two destroyers as well as a number of armed trawlers. This same flotilla, operating out of Cherbourg, had at the end of February achieved the first E-boat success of the year by sinking the 4,850-ton freighter *Moldavia* in Lyme Bay. Now, in spite of the presence of destroyers, they mounted an attack on the six ships of the convoy, managing to torpedo and sink the 1,740-ton steamer *Stanlake*. The destroyers moved in to intercept, at which point two of the E-boats (*S.65* commanded by Oberleutnant Walter Sobottka and *S.112* commanded by Kapitän-leutnant Karl Müller) turned on one of them – the *Eskdale* of the Royal Norwegian Navy – and sank her after scoring simultaneous hits with their torpedoes.

These three ships sunk by the 5th Flotilla were the only E-boat successes in the first half of the year. The superiority of the defence over the attack was illustrated on the night of 28-29 March when a strong force of seven E-boats tried to attack the southbound Convoy FS1074 off Smith's Knoll, a shallow area of water at the northern end of E-boat Alley. Gunfire from the escort destroyers was just too much for the E-boats which had to turn away without accomplishing their mission, unable to penetrate the defensive screen. However, another factor in the fighting that year was a sharp rise in the number of engagements fought by opposing craft, as attacking and defending boats met in the convoy routes on either side of the North Sea or English Channel, or clashed somewhere mid-way between. This was the situation on the night in question, where on patrol in the Smith's Knoll area and waiting for just such a move by the enemy were two Fairmile 'C' MGBs, *33* and *321*, under the command of Lt Donald Gould Bradford RNR who was to prove himself one of the most daring and successful coastal craft leaders. He set off in pursuit of the E-boats and suddenly came upon a group of five of them, moving slowly at about 12 knots while they considered whether to return home or launch another attack. Although not equipped with the distinctive torpedo tubes, the Fairmiles were as similar in outline to the E-boats as any of the British craft. The night was pitch black with visibility little more than a hundred yards – the main reason, in fact, why the Germans had ventured out on this occasion – and the E-boats assumed that the MGBs were the remaining two of their number making for the rendezvous point. Bradford brought his craft to within forty yards of the enemy, then opened fire with every available gun. As previous battles had shown, it was very difficult to set fire to the steel-hulled German boats. But one of the enemy suddenly exploded and erupted with a belch of flame, probably caused by an Oerlikon shell hitting the warhead of a spare torpedo. Three of the E-boats sped away with Bradford's partner in pursuit, although he failed to catch up with them due to their greater speed. Bradford was left on his own with one E-boat on fire and most of her gunners killed, but now under fire himself from the lead boat. He turned and cut across her wake, trying an old Coastal Forces dodge of dropping a depth charge under her stern. This did not succeed, but he then found himself going at full speed and only some forty yards from her port side. Both boats were exchanging a murderous fire when Bradford suddenly decided to ram the enemy. He rang ramming stations on the gun bells, ordered the helmsman to put the wheel hard over, and struck the enemy about twenty feet from the stern. The MGB rode up over the E-boat, then came down again as the enemy's hull broke. The stern section slid away as the MGB continued forward, Bradford found that he had in fact sliced clean through. The E-boat in question, *S.29*, was later scuttled by the Germans after her survivors had been rescued.

In many ways, the Germans were now in a position similar to that of Britain in 1940, their coastal traffic facing constant attack from superior forces. The difference was that at least Britain had taken the necessary steps to build up Coastal Forces, whereas the Germans were now suffering from a serious decline in the number of new E-boats coming from the shipyards, for which inter-departmental jealousies in Naval Command and a lack of proper planning were largely responsible. As it happened, in spite of the forces ranged against them in 1943, it was remarkable how relatively few E-boats were actually lost, as distinct from claims that were made in good faith but later proved to be unfounded. This applied also in the case of MTBs, and a feature of small boat fighting throughout the war was the ability of craft on both sides to struggle back to base in spite of severe damage and having been assumed by the opposition to have sunk.

During the whole of 1943 the Germans lost only 14 E-boats – six in actions with destroyers and MGBs, two mine casualties, three in attacks by aircraft when caught out in the open during daylight, and three in an RAF bombing raid on Kiel. Nevertheless, they could ill afford such losses. By September, none of the five flotillas operating in the western area was at full strength; the 2nd and 6th at Ostend had only seven and five boats respectively, the 4th at Boulogne six boats, the 5th at Cherbourg five boats, and the 8th at Ijmuiden three boats. Against these, the strength and disposition of British Coastal Forces in home waters was 39 MTBs, 47 MGBs and 32 MLs in Nore Command; 24 MTBs, 13 MGBs and 9 MLs in Dover Command; 30 MTBs, 6 SGBs, 14 MGBs and 56 MLs in Portsmouth Command; and 8 MTBs, 21 MGBs and 25 MLs in Plymouth Command.

The parallel with Britain's situation in 1940 was equally apparent as regards air operations. As stated earlier, it was direct attack by German aircraft, and air minelaying even more, that caused the greatest damage to British coastal convoys in the early years of the war and posed the most serious threat. Had the Luftwaffe continued these operations, it is questionable whether Britain could have continued to fight the war. But the opportunity had been frittered away in erratic changes of policy and failure to construct the right types of aircraft, much of the responsibility for which could be laid at Hitler's door. Now the chance had gone forever.

Not a single British coastal vessel was lost to the Luftwaffe in 1943, in spite of some 7,000 sorties flown, and the RAF lost only seventeen aircraft in its day and night defence of shipping. Total British losses in home waters for the year were only 25 ships of some 52,400 tons, of which E-boats were responsible for seven ships totalling about 16,500 tons, the remainder being due to mines. This was only a tiny fraction of the amount of shipping that passed in and out of the Thames alone in 1943, which totalled no less than 36 million tons.

On the other hand, German coastal shipping was beginning to suffer heavily as a result of a great combined operation involving all the RAF and Naval Commands. The Strike Wing of Coastal Command's No 16 Group, equipped mostly with Beaufighters armed with torpedoes, bombs, 20mm cannon and the new rocket projectile and often escorted by Spitfires of Fighter Command, was responsible for attacks against the strongly escorted convoys moving along the North Sea coast of Holland. The successes achieved led to a sharp decline in the traffic moving in and out of Rotterdam; this was by far the most convenient port for the discharge of iron ore from Norway and Sweden required by the Ruhr industries, but sensitivity of the Swedes to losses of their merchant ships forced the Germans to make greater use of Emdem, putting a considerable strain on their inland transportation system. Coastal Command's No 18 Group, flying mostly Hampdens and Mosquitoes, was responsible for operations off the Norwegian coast, while the long-range Mitchells and

SHORT SUNDERLAND Mk II

Whirlwinds of No 19 Group kept a watch in the Bay of Biscay for iron ore shipments from Spain. In addition to providing fighter escorts for bombing missions, Fighter Command had the responsibility for attacking the enemy's coastal shipping in the English Channel, flying Hurricane-bombers and Albacore torpedo-bombers lent by the Fleet Air Arm. In all these operations, aircraft worked in close co-operation with the Navy's surface vessels, including Coastal Forces. It was of mutual benefit; thus, reconnaissance flights by Coastal Command could inform the MTBs of suitable targets while fighter cover enabled the boats to return safely during the hours of daylight, so that they could operate further afield and for longer periods. On the other hand, a 'flak' ship sunk in the North Sea by MTBs or MGBs meant that much less danger to the night bombers on their missions over Germany.

Direct attacks by British aircraft against German shipping in the Home Theatre during 1943 led to the sinking of 50 ships totalling some 90,000 tons – and damage to many more – for the loss of 209 aircraft. Among the German losses were three E-boats: *S.75* and *S.121* sunk by Spitfires in the Channel on 4 March and 4 August respectively, and *S.74* which was scuttled in the North Sea after an attack by Beaufighters on 5 November. But the greatest British success was in minelaying, as the Germans had found earlier. The first British acoustic mines had been introduced in September 1942; now a highly effective combined acoustic and magnetic firing-mechanism was developed. Britain's minesweeping force was now more than sufficient to cope with the declining number of mines being laid by German E-boats and aircraft, and more concerted efforts could be made to lay mines off the enemy's coast. Coastal Force ML flotillas played an important role in this, making frequent sorties to place mines in the enemy's swept channels and at the entrances of harbours, but the great majority were laid by Bomber Command, whose Wellingtons, Halifaxes, Stirlings and Lancasters flew continual missions along the whole of the

Short Sunderland Mk II of No. 10 Squadron RAAF, No. 19 Group Coastal Command, Mount Batten, Plymouth, UK, April 1942

Another of the old RN destroyers modified for coastal escort duties, HMS Whitshed was further adapted in 1944 for anti-E-boat work when a twin 6-pounder replaced one of three 4.7inch guns and radar was installed so that MGBs could be vectored on to E-boats

enemy-occupied coast from the Bay of Biscay to the North Sea coast of Germany. They laid more than 14,000 mines during the year, losing 155 aircraft in the process. But 143 enemy ships were destroyed by this means, totalling 104,000 tons. Thus, more ships were sunk and fewer aircraft lost than in direct attacks on shipping. The effectiveness of air mine-laying, as the Germans should have realised earlier, was one of the most revealing lessons of the war. But the Germans had failed to press home their advantage, and now Britain turned the tables with a vengeance.

As usual, during the short summer months which did not leave sufficient time for the E-boats to return home before daylight, there was a lull in their offensive operations in the North Sea. This did not mean they were idle, however. To counter the growing British offensive against coastal shipping off the Dutch coast and in the Channel, most of them joined with destroyers, torpedo boats and other craft on convoy escort duties, protecting in particular the blockade-runners which were bringing vital iron ore from Spain to French ports now that the Swedish Government had become reluctant to charter its own merchant ships to Germany for carrying ore from Swedish mines. Along the whole of the German-occupied coastline from Brittany to the Frisian islands this was a period of fast-moving night encounters in which large numbers of craft on both sides – destroyers, E-boats, MTBs, MGBs, armed trawlers, minelayers, minesweepers, and many other types – were involved in individual battles which were usually confused and often lasted several hours, spread over a wide area. Losses were sustained on both sides but these were usually among escort craft on the one hand and MTBs and MGBs on the other, with the balance about even. It was seldom that an MTB could penetrate a convoy's defensive screen to score a torpedo hit on a merchantman, just as the E-boats found when they went on the offensive. Sometimes the heavy gun batteries on either side of the Dover Strait joined in, but to little effect.

The E-boat attacks were resumed in the autumn, and on 5 August the armed trawler *Redgauntlet* was sunk off Harwich, followed on 25 September by another trawler, the *Franc Tireur*, in the same area. During the second action one of the E-boats, *S.96*, was sunk after being rammed in turn by two MLs, *145* and *150*, whose commanders followed Lt Bradford's earlier lead in concluding that the only way to make sure of sinking an E-boat was to ram her. The Germans had now devised a startling new form of tactics, planned in great secrecy during the summer, in which a large number of E-boats combined in one sortie rather than attacking a few at a time in different areas. For the operation on 25 September, three flotillas took part. And then, on the night of 24-25 October no fewer than 28 boats from the 2nd, 4th, 6th and 8th Flotillas set out in the biggest massed E-boat attack of the war. This force, gathered together at Ijmuiden for the purpose, constituted almost the whole of the E-boat strength in the western area at that time. Its objective was the northbound Convoy FN 1160 off Cromer on the Norfolk coast. But the result showed only too clearly how far the British had come in perfecting their defensive measures.

The convoy was escorted by no fewer than five destroyers, while six 'D' class MGBs and two MLs were on patrol some ten miles offshore with two MTBs on stand-by in Lowestoft. By the time the E-boats, led by Kapitän-leutnant Werner Lützow in *S.88*, had divided as planned into divisions of four or six boats each about 12 miles off the convoy route, their presence had been detected by a force of RAF bombers returning from a raid on Germany. The convoy was warned, and in the meantime, anticipating that the E-boats would go back the same way they had come, namely the direct route from Ijmuiden north of the Ower Bank, Nore Command laid plans to cut off their line of retreat. The destroyer *Pytchley*, guarding the seaward flank of the convoy, was the first to make contact with the E-boats after picking up a unit of six on her radar. She drove them off to the north-east, severely damaging one; as was realised later, this action saved the convoy from being accurately located. Two of the MGBs – *609* and *610* under Lt P. Edge – were sent to intercept, while MGBs *603* and *607* under Lt R.M. Marshall were sent to cut off their line of retirement to Ijmuiden, together with the fast MTBs from Lowestoft, *439* and *442* under the Canadian Lt C.A. Burk. The destroyer *Eglinton* was ordered to remain with the convoy while the remaining three were also sent north to help the MGBs.

Splitting the E-boats into several small groups was an ingenious idea and would have posed a dangerous threat had it not been for the lucky chance that the convoy was two hours ahead of its schedule. When the E-boats reached the shipping route, they were well astern of the convoy. Only a straggling trawler remained unguarded, the *William Steven*, and she was easily sunk by torpedo. However, it was the only German success of that night. In the meantime, the destroyers *Worcester* and *Mackay* had engaged several groups of E-boats in action and *Mackay* had severely damaged one boat, *S.63*. As a result, the E-boats were driven further northwards to where the MGBs were waiting. The unit under Lt Marshall intercepted a group which included *S.63*, unable to make more than about 20 knots. Senior Officer Lützow in *S.88* made smoke and attempted to hold off the MGBs while the crippled boat tried to escape, but in doing so he took terrible punishment from the concentrated fire of the two MGBs. He himself was killed and his boat set on fire. Marshall left to chase *S.63* and delivered the *coup de grâce* by ramming her. Shortly afterwards, *S.88* blew up.

When the confused events of that night were pieced together, it became apparent that 16 separate actions had been fought. But none of the British boats had been sunk, as against two of the enemy, which was a high price to pay for the destruction of one small trawler. However, this did not deter the E-boats. Just over a week later, on 2 November, units of the 5th Flotilla had better success when they moved to the eastern Channel for the first time since 1941 and sank three freighters southwest of Dungeness, taking the escorts by surprise. Two nights later the 6th Flotilla, while actually on a minelaying mission, sank by torpedo two ships of Convoy FN1170 between Cromer and Great Yarmouth; it was while on its way back to base that this flotilla was attacked by Beaufighters and *S.74* destroyed.

One of the long-standing complaints among the E-boat crews was that although their craft were faster than most of the British, they suffered from being less heavily armed. This was certainly true as far as the new D-type MGBs were concerned, armed as they were with 2-pounders (either a Vickers Pom-Pom or a Rolls-Royce type) in addition to twin 20mm cannon and twin .5inch machine-guns. Again this was a complete turnabout from the early years of the war when it was the British boats which carried inferior armament. However, during the winter of 1943-44, most of the German boats were re-armed with 40mm or 37mm AA guns in addition to the 20mm Oerlikons, and this brought about a new aggressive spirit among the German forces, to the point where they actually began to seek out and pursue MTBs rather than avoiding action as before. A change of tactics was also called for in view of the greatly improved British defensive measures, which now included the installation of radar equipment in destroyers and MGBs as well as the shore-based radar network. Instead of continuing the previous method of lying in wait on convoy routes, where there was now every chance of their presence being detected by radar, the E-boats developed hit-and-run tactics, without trying to disguise their intentions but making use of their superior speed to attack and then retire out of range of the destroyers. If any British boats pursued them, they would lead them towards their own coast, then turn abruptly and the hunters would become the hunted. It was in such a way that one of the most brilliant MTB commanders, Lt Derek Leaf DSC, was killed in the early hours of 15 February 1944.

FIGHT TO THE END

The action that led to Leaf's death began on the evening of 14 February when a group of six E-boats crossed the North Sea with the intention of laying mines off the east coast. They were detected by shore radar, however, and driven off by the Harwich-based corvettes *Mallard* and *Shearwater* which were on patrol. Meanwhile, five MTBs under Leaf's command were sent to the southern end of Brown Ridge to intercept the E-boats on their return home. But the British boats were too late; the enemy were already ahead of them. So Leaf decided to pursue them to Ijmuiden.

On approaching the Dutch coast, although they did not realise it at the time, the MTBs were themselves being hunted by the E-boats which had turned back, having expected to be followed. Before contact was made, the MTBs came upon an enemy flak ship and two trawlers. Leaf's *MTB.444*, together with *MTB.455* commanded by the New Zealander Lt M.V. Round, made a combined attack in which the flak ship was torpedoed and one of the trawlers repeatedly hit by gunfire and left burning. However, the second trawler managed to hit *444* heavily both above and below the water line. Its fire raked the bridge and Leaf was killed instantly, together with his Petty Officer and two ratings. Meanwhile, the other three MTBs had regrouped and in Leaf's absence, although it was not then realised what had happened, the Canadian Lt C.A. Burk took over as Senior Officer. As he set off to search for the two missing boats he had the shock of discovering by radar that six E-boats were shadowing his unit 1,000 yards off on the port quarter. Further radar contacts picked up more E-boats ahead. Burk decided to attack the shadowing boats first. He altered course to port and, followed by the rest of his unit, crossed the bows of the leading E-boat at full speed, no more than 100 yards off. Fire was exchanged between all the craft, and then general confusion developed in which the three MTBs were outnumbered by an estimated

17 E-boats, but it became difficult for either side to distinguish between friend and foe. In such actions, it was almost impossible for one small craft to sink another unless by an extremely lucky shot. Eventually the three MTBs broke off the engagement and returned to base, where they found that the other two MTBs had already arrived and learned for the first time that Leaf had been killed. In spite of the fire that had been exchanged with the E-boats, the only other casualties were three men slightly wounded in Burk's boat.

By early 1944 the Luftwaffe was practically non-existent over the narrow seas, not only failing to protect its own coastal shipping but doing little to hinder the enormous forces being assembled for the Allied invasion of Europe. The German offensive in these waters was left almost entirely to the E-boats. Although the flotillas operating in the western area were joined by one more – the 9th (Kapitänleutnant von Mirbach) – this advantage was lost when the 6th was withdrawn for service in the Baltic. The five flotillas were seriously depleted with no more than about 30 craft operational at any one time as against a nominal strength of 60; the advantage in equipment was also undoubtedly with the Allied flotillas, especially in radar. Nevertheless, the E-boat crews were experienced and stubborn fighters and had no intention of slackening off, in spite of being let down by the Luftwaffe. German coastal shipping had declined at this time; whereas that of the British had increased considerably, added to which there was a large-scale movement of Allied forces along the southern coasts in preparation for D-Day. All this gave the E-boats ample opportunity to choose targets from among half-a-dozen convoys moving slowly along the east and south coasts at any one time. By switching rapidly from one area of attack to another, they were occasionally able to achieve some unpleasant surprises. Operating out of Cherbourg, together with the 9th Flotilla, units of the 5th Flotilla sank three freighters and the trawler *Wallasey* out of Convoy WP457 in the western Channel on the night of 5-6 January, and repeated this success on the 31st of the month by sinking two freighters and a trawler out of Convoy CW243 off Beachy Head. An even more dramatic achievement came on the night of 28 April when the two flotillas operated together to attack a convoy of American landing ships (LSTs) in Lyme Bay, sinking three with the loss of nearly 200 naval personnel and 441 soldiers.

In the context of total coastal shipping and movements, of course, these losses could well have been greater. Also, the Germans had to pay an increasingly heavy penalty for such operations. As British Coastal Forces had found, it was extremely difficult to control a force of fast-moving craft at night; on occasion, shots were exchanged between friendly craft, and collisions were frequent, the latter being responsible for the loss of two E-boats early in the year, *S.94* and *S.128*. Bombing raids on enemy ports now being carried out mainly by the heavy bombers of the Eighth US Army Air Force, were responsible for further losses, such as the destruc tion of *S.93* and *S.129* during an attack by Marauders on Ijmuiden on 29 March. During actions at sea, the French destroyer *La Combattante* sank two E-boats, *S.147* on 26 April and *S.141* on 13 May, which were among boats sent out from Boulogne on reconnaissance to discover where the Allied landing craft were concentrating for the forthcoming invasion. Included among those lost on the latter boat was one of Admiral Dönitz's two sons, a German naval lieutenant. In the Channel, it was one of the main functions of Fighter Command to harass the E-boats on their missions to lay minefields as a defence against invasion. Night patrols were instituted, using the slow Albacores which were ideally suited to the purpose, together with Swordfish and Avengers which were also lent by the Fleet Air Arm. In this way, on 19 May, *S.87* was sunk off Orfordness by Swordfish of 819 Squadron.

Meanwhile, MTBs and MGBs were stepping up their offensive sweeps against German shipping, from the Norwegian coast in the north, down along the Dutch coast, through the Dover Strait and English Channel, and westwards as far as the Channel Islands and off the coast of Brittany. The results were not always so successful as those claimed at the time, and a number of MTBs were lost – about the same, in fact, as E-boat losses in British waters. But Coastal Forces played a vital role in achieving that degree of maritime control over the narrow seas which was essential for when the great invasion fleets set sail for France.

Throughout the four years of fighting by Coastal Forces, most of the action had been in the North Sea. Now it was the English Channel which came into prominence with the biggest invasion the world had ever seen, the Normandy landings, in which small fighting craft had many important tasks assigned to them. Since the invasion was to be launched principally by Portsmouth Command, a Captain of Coastal Forces in the Channel was appointed (Capt P.V. McLaughlin) to take charge of all MTB and ML operations within the Command. (From this point on, MGBs were no longer designated separately.) Included among his small staff to make detailed plans were such experienced flotilla commanders as Christopher Dreyer and Peter Scott. In addition, American PT-boats made their first appearance in British waters, brought over in the first instance at the urgent request of the Office of Strategic Services to land and pick up agents on the French coast. This led to the re-commissioning of Squadron 2 which had previously been wound up in the Solomons at the end of 1943. The first of the Higgins boats, under Lt-Cdr John Bulkeley, arrived at Dartmouth in April, fitted with special navigational equipment to help them in their cloak-and-dagger operations. The first of these took place on the night of 19 May, when *PT.71* landed a party of agents within 500 yards of German sentries, and similar missions continued up until November; the crews never knew the identity of their passengers and never once made contact with the enemy, which was exactly as intended. Meanwhile, further PT squadrons were shipped across from the United States to take part in the invasion itself – Squadron 34 (Lt Allen H. Harris), Squadron 35 (Lt-Cdr Richard Davis Jr) and Squadron 30 (Lt Robert L. Searles). Bulkeley was appointed as task group commander of all PT operations.

The main job of the British and American craft was to help guard the flanks of the spearhead attack on the shores of the Baie de la Seine, and then to protect the subsequent flow of cross-Channel traffic. The most likely attacks were expected to come from destroyers, torpedo boats, and minesweepers, of which the Germans still had large forces based in the Low Countries and on the Atlantic coast of France, and from E-boats based along the coast from Cherbourg to Ijmuiden.

In the meantime, knowing that the invasion was imminent, the Germans were preparing their own plans, in which E-boats were also to play an important part.

Petersen, as commander of all E-boats in the Channel and North Sea, with his headquarters at Scheveningen, strove desperately to get as many boats as he could into operational order. At the time the invasion began on 6 June, he had 34 boats available, with five more under repair; it was not until later in June that the 6th Flotilla was brought back from the Baltic to aid his efforts. Against these were some 76 British MTBs and 36 American PTs included in a total Allied force of more than 1,200 warships and over 4,000 landing craft. The E-boat crews, as tenacious as always, did what they could to stem this mighty tide, but they had little chance. Thus began a period which saw their most severe losses of the war.

On the morning of the invasion, both the 4th Flotilla at Boulogne and the 5th at Le Havre tried to leave their concrete-sheltered bases to attack the invasion fleet, but they were beaten back by the tremendous Allied air attack by bombers and fighter-bombers. Only Mirbach's 9th Flotilla at Cherbourg managed to put to sea, but was immediately repelled by a curtain of defensive fire from the escorting warships. The E-boats were forced to return to harbour and there they remained throughout the first day, anxiously following the news of the battles taking place on the beaches. With the Luftwaffe entirely absent there was little the German Navy could do to prevent the Allied landings in Normandy. The only warships that approached the invasion fleet at all that morning were three 'Möwe' class torpedo boats from Le Harvre, which attacked one of the exposed flanks of, and managed to sink the Norwegian destroyer *Svenner*. From the naval point of view the invasion went precisely according to plan, with the enemy first taken by surprise and then demoralized by the sheer weight and strength of Allied forces; it was only when the assault troops reached the obstacle-covered beaches that the fighting began. By the end of the first day it was clear that the landings themselves had gone better than almost anyone would have dared hope.

However, such a situation could not last for long, and as the initial surprise wore off, the Germans began to counter-attack the vital Allied supply route across the Channel. The E-boats played an important part in this, based as they were at Cherbourg and Le Havre on either side of the bridgehead. They were out in the early hours of 7 June, when no fewer than seven clashes with MTBs occurred. The 55th Flotilla under Lt-Cdr Bradford and the Canadian 29th Flotilla under Lt-Cdr Anthony Law bore the brunt of that night's fighting, in which one German R-boat blew up after hitting a mine, two MTBs were damaged, and the E-boats succeeded in sinking a landing ship in Seine Bay. And thus began a series of nightly battles that grew in intensity, with the Germans concentrating their main attack against the British eastern flank. This was primarily because most of the German destroyers and light craft were based at Le Havre, the more heavily defended port. In fact, losses amongst the Cherbourg-based E-boats were so high during the first week of the invasion that the remainder were transferred to Le Havre, where the fight in the Channel centred after the fall of Cherbourg to American troops on 26 June. On the strongly defended American western flank of the supply route, where it was seldom possible for enemy craft to penetrate the defensive screen, the PT-boats had no contact at all with E-boats from the start of the invasion up until August when they were withdrawn from the Normandy area, some to be transferred to operate in the vicinity of the Channel Islands while others were attached to Portsmouth to work with British Coastal Forces patrolling the eastern flank.

Considering the enormous number of targets available to them, the E-boats achieved only a moderate success. During the first week, out of the great mass of Allied shipping in Seine Bay, they sank only two American landing ships, six smaller British landing craft, two tugs, two

Part of the large barrage balloon force which served to protect the Allied Expeditionary Fleet steaming across the English Channel for the D-Day landings on the Normandy coast on 6th June 1944

MTBs, the frigate *Halstead* whose bows were blown off by a torpedo, and three small freighters of a convoy south of the Isle of Wight. Three boats of the 5th Flotilla were lost – *S.136* in action and *139* and *140* sunk by mines – but even worse was to come. On 13 June, Beaufighters scored a notable success by sinking four boats of the 2nd Flotilla in an attack off Le Touquet. Shortly after dusk of the following day, the E-boats suffered their heaviest-ever single loss when eleven were destroyed and three damaged in a massive air raid on Le Havre by Lancasters of Bomber Command. Among those killed was Kurt Johannsen, commander of the 5th Flotilla. The 6th Flotilla was moved back from the Baltic to make up for these disastrous losses, but the E-boats caused no further damage to Allied craft during June. In his appreciation for the work of Coastal Forces, meanwhile, the naval commander of the Eastern Task Force stated that it was largely due to their efforts that the invasion area had been kept virtually free from surface attack.

When the Germans began their final evacuation of Cherbourg at the end of the month, the MTBs had a chance to renew their offensive after so many days of defensive patrols. Two groups of the 14th MTB Flotilla were waiting outside the harbour for the departure of the last convoy. The first group of three boats, under Lt G.H. Baker, caught the convoy as it was forming up and sank by torpedo two coasters, a trawler and a tug. Then the second group came in, led by the Senior Officer of the flotilla, Lt D.A. Shaw, and sank at least two more vessels.

With the help of reinforcements the number of E-boats operating from Le Havre, Dieppe and Boulogne totalled 20 by the beginning of July, and these continued to make nightly forays against the cross-Channel convoys. Patrols of destroyers, frigates and coastal craft were kept constantly on the alert, with aircraft of Coastal Command and the Fleet Air Arm watching the enemy's bases and attacking whenever a target appeared. However, the E-boats operated only in small groups now, having too few boats to risk a mass attack as before, and then only during the hours of darkness. They remained elusive targets, and in spite of the encounters that took place, it was seldom that an E-boat was sunk at sea. The battles fought between the fast-moving craft were generally confused and inconclusive, typified by the actions that took place in the Baie de la Seine on the night of 26-27 July in which a succession of collisions resulted in the loss of two British MTBs and one E-boat (*S.182*). On the other hand, Coastal Forces managed to prevent the E-boats breaking through to attack the shipping that was bringing over some 17,000 tons of supplies a day to the British assault alone. The enemy had better success against the less heavily guarded coastal convoys that were continuing to move to and fro along the south coast; on the last day of July, E-boats sank a steamer off Beachy Head and torpedoed and damaged four other ships including the frigate *Trollope*.

In August the E-boats were equipped with a new long-range circling torpedo, the 'Dackel'; although its speed was only 9 knots, it could run straight for about 16 miles and then circle for another 18 miles, with a total running time of no less than 3½ hours. This would have been virtually useless in normal circumstances but it posed a more serious threat against an anchorage crowded with shipping The cruiser *Frobisher* and two other ships were damaged and a landing craft sunk by this means. Two other 'secret weapons' also made their first appearance at this time, the 'Marder' which was a torpedo guided by a frogman who sat astride it, and the 'Linsen', a motor-boat filled with explosive and aimed at a target by the operator who jumped clear at the last minute. These were responsible for sinking the destroyer *Quorn* together with a trawler and a landing craft, but most were destroyed by MTBs and other ships before they could get near enough to do any damage. Such measures, calling for considerable bravery on the part of the men concerned, showed how desperate the Germans had become in trying to hold back the remorseless tide of troops and equipment crossing the Channel.

Towards the end of August, while a full-scale assault on Le Havre was made by Canadian troops from the landward side, MTBs joined with destroyers and frigates to establish a close blockade of the approaches to the port. This was the most eventful period of all for Coastal Forces in this area, involving continual night engagements as the Germans tried to move in supplies and reinforcements by sea and then to evacuate their shipping in strongly escorted convoys. The E-boats played their part in this, but were unable to prevent heavy losses and several of the craft themselves were lost. German resistance in the Channel ports was stubborn – indeed, the garrison at Dunkirk did not surrender until the end of the war – but with the final evacuation from Le Havre on 1 September, all maritime opposition in these waters ended. German shipping, including the dozen E-boats which were all that remained of Petersen's original force of 34 at the start of the invasion, was driven through the Dover Strait and into the North Sea for temporary shelter in bases on the Belgian and Dutch coasts. The eastern end of the Channel was cleared of the enemy for the first time in four years. During that last momentous week, Allied naval forces including MTBs and PTs had sunk nine armed landing craft, five coasters, two trawlers, two R-boats and one E-boat, with several more E-boats so badly damaged that they were no longer serviceable. From D-Day until the end of August, MTBs alone claimed 34 craft sunk and nine possibles, for the loss of ten to themselves, three in action with E-boats and the remainder by mines and collisions. The E-boats sank 11 vessels and damaged eight others but lost 22, mostly by bombing although the last casualty fell to the coastal gun batteries at Dover.

In the western area, where a flotilla each of SGBs and 'D' class MTBs had been attached to Admiral Kirk's Task Force to reinforce his four PT squadrons, there had been few actions during the early days of the invasion and no contact with E-boats. These units with the exception of two PT squadrons (30 and 35) which were transferred to Portsmouth, then joined the Coastal Force operations from Plymouth and Dartmouth off the Brittany coast and among the Channel Islands. Their exploits were so successful that enemy traffic among the islands was brought virtually to a standstill by the time that the enemy garrisons on St Malo and Ile de Cezembre fell on 18 August. From that point onwards, the Channel Islands ceased to be of any military importance. Meanwhile, Coastal Forces continued to operate off the French ports to the east until the night of 1-2 October, when the last action was fought between Boulogne and Calais. Most of the flotillas were then transferred to the North Sea where the E-boats were now fighting the last desperate stage in the battle for the narrow seas. It is worth recording that from the beginning of the war until September 1944, when the Germans were cleared from the Channel, no less than 2,000 convoys of over 45,000 ships had sailed from the key

Preceded and flanked by MGBs, E-boats make their way across the English Channel to Portsmouth after their surrender at the end of the war

assembly and terminal point at Southend.

Having re-grouped at Rotterdam and Ijmuiden, the E-boats now resumed their main task of laying mines on the east coast convoy routes and off the Belgian coast. But they were also used occasionally to ship supplies to the beleaguered German garrison at Dunkirk. A new flotilla was formed at this time – the 10th commanded by Kapitänleutnant Karl Müller – and its first mission on the night of 18-19 September was to make one of the Dunkirk runs. The three boats of the flotilla that were operational – *S.183, S.200* and *S.702* – were to cover four other boats loaded with stores and ammunition. These supplies were landed successfully but then the covering force was detected by the radar-fitted frigate *Stayner*, on patrol with two 'D' class MTBs of the 64th Flotilla commanded by Lt-Cdr D. Wilkie – *MTB.724* (Lt J.F. Humphreys) and *MTB.728* (Lt F.N. Thomson). The patrol system of combining a ship equipped with radar and MTBs which could be vectored towards a target had been used defensively in 1943 for convoy protection off the east coast; now it was being employed offensively against E-boats off the enemy's coast. *Stayner* gave the MTBs the course to steer and herself moved in to provide support with her guns. All three E-boats were sunk, two by the MTBs and one by the frigate, and 60 survivors taken prisoner including Müller himself.

In spite of losses such as these, the Germans managed to bring their total E-boat strength in the North Sea up to about twenty by mid-October, largely due to the efforts of the workshops in repairing damaged craft. Their main missions were to lay mines off the east coast and occasionally in the eastern Channel. But the Allied patrols were more alert than ever, and in the battles which raged in the familiar area around Smith's Knoll, the MTBs invariably came off best. The E-boats sank no ships at all in October and their only success in November was one small tanker off Ostend. In December, raids by RAF Bomber Command on the E-boat base at Ijmuiden resulted in the destruction of three craft, and on the night of 22-23, two more were sunk by MTBs during an unsuccessful attack on a convoy off the Scheldt Estuary.

By early 1945, with the war in Europe coming irrevocably to its conclusion, there began a gradual reduction in the overall strength of Britain's Coastal Forces. There was still plenty of work for the MTBs to do, of course, and the flotillas operating out of Lerwick in particular found no lack of targets off the coast of Norway; in the five months up to mid-February they sank nine merchant vessels (eight by torpedo and one by gunfire), six trawlers, two minesweepers and one E-boat. However, there no longer seemed any need for the very large force of MTBs that had been built up by this time. Building programmes were cancelled, older boats paid off, the American PT squadrons disbanded, and a number of bases closed down. It appeared that for coastal craft in the North Sea the war was as good as over. But the Germans had still not played their last card. Just as on land the German Army was still capable of springing an

unpleasant surprise with its counter-attack in the Ardennes, so in the narrow seas the E-boats showed they were still a force to be reckoned with.

Although the great port of Antwerp had been captured virtually intact on 4 September, it could not be used as an entry for supplies and reinforcements until the Germans had been cleared from their strongly fortified positions on the islands in the estuary to the River Scheldt. This was not accomplished until early November, by a combined operation including Canadian and Royal Marine Commandos, and it was not until the end of the month that the eighty miles of river up to Antwerp had been cleared of mines. Convoys from the Thames to Antwerp started in December and by the beginning of 1945 acquired an even greater importance in view of the need to supply the Allied armies preparing their drive to the Rhine and also to replace the equipment lost in holding back the German offensive in the Ardennes. However, almost the whole of western Holland was still in German hands, and this included the E-boat bases at Ijmuiden, Rotterdam and Den Helder. The Germans were not slow in taking advantage of the targets now offered virtually on their own doorstep, namely the vital convoys passing up the River Scheldt to Antwerp. Another E-boat flotilla was brought back from the Baltic and the existing flotillas reinforced once again, so that about thirty craft were operational. For this last major offensive in the North Sea, the E-boats were aided by another 'secret weapon' in the midget submarines ('Seehunden') that had been developed.

The surrendered E-boats arrive at HMS Hornet, the Coastal Forces base at Portsmouth

One of the E-boats which surrendered at the end of the war, flying the white flag. About 100 of these craft survived the war and were divided among the victors. In 1957, the Royal Navy handed two of them back to the Federal Germany Navy which for several years used them for training purposes

Throwing caution to the winds the E-boats came out on every possible occasion at night in groups of six or eight to make torpedo attacks at sea and to lay mines in the Scheldt. During January and February E-boats and midget submarines were responsible for sinking seven ships by torpedo, while mines laid by E-boats sank a further 15 ships of 36,000 tons. Extra destroyers and MTBs had to be called in to meet this threat and in a series of fierce clashes sank four of the E-boats. In spite of the personal bravery of the Seehund crews, the two-man midget submarines did not come up to German expectations; of the 80 captured or sunk at this time, Coastal Forces accounted for 23. Had it not been for the strength of the British surface and air patrols, however, they would have achieved a considerable success in attacks on convoys.

The Germans stepped up their attacks in March, with the E-boats out almost every night and switching their operations abruptly from Dutch waters to the east coast of England in an effort to take the convoys by surprise. They were invariably driven off, only managing one important success by torpedo during the month, when on the night of 18-19 March they slipped through the defensive screen around Convoy FS 1759 off Lowestoft and sank the freighters *Crichtoun* and *Rogate*. In fact, these were the last Allied merchant ships in World War II to be sunk by E-boats in a direct attack. However, the mines laid by these craft continued to take their toll, and a further eleven ships were lost in this way during the month. Three E-boats were lost, including *S.181* which was sunk by a Beaufighter off Den Helder on 21-22 March, the commander of the 2nd Flotilla (Korvettenkapitän Opdenhoff) being among those killed.

It was during the period of one week in April that the E-boats were finally beaten, largely due to the close co-operation which by then existed between Allied air and surface patrols in which a major factor was the development of airborne radar; by this means, Coastal Command aircraft could detect enemy craft almost as soon as they left base and track them until MTBs were in a position to make contact. Fittingly, perhaps, that final week saw a peak in the intensity of fighting between E-boats and MTBs which had seldom been equalled before. It began on the night of 6-7 April when a unit of three MTBs under Lt J. May intercepted a group of five E-boats of the 2nd Flotilla, making what was to be its final mining operation. After a desperate running battle, the honours were even with two E-boats (*S.176* and *S.177*) and two MTBs (*494* and *5001*) lost. The manner of these losses graphically illustrates the kind of encounters that took place in the latter stages of the war. Lt May's own boat and one of the enemy were both sunk after colliding with one another. Another MTB commanded by Lt Foster sank a second E-boat by ramming, but then had to be written off after hitting the floating wreckage of May's boat. On the following night, a further two E-boats (*S.202* and *S.703*) were sunk in a collision with each other after they had been severely damaged by gunfire from an MTB patrol led by Lt Dixon. A third boat, *S.223*, was blown up by a mine off Ostend. The final action between E-boats and Coastal Forces took place five nights later, on 12-13 April, when the patrolling frigate *Ekins* and two MTBs intercepted a group on its way to lay mines in the Scheldt Estuary. One of the E-boats was badly damaged before they had to return to base with their mission unaccomplished. There were by then still 15 E-boats operational, but that was the last time they put to sea before the end of the war. The losses they had suffered in the final stages were just too heavy for the meagre results being achieved, and added to that there was a critical shortage of fuel and disorganisation at their bases due to continual bombing raids.

Only on one last occasion did two of the E-boats make the journey across the North Sea again. That was on 13 May, following Germany's unconditional surrender, when they sailed under a white flag from Rotterdam to Felixstowe, bringing with them representatives of the German Naval Command who were to inform Nore Command of the location of German minefields. The two E-boats were under the command of Korvettenkapitän Fimmen who had taken over the 4th Flotilla after the death of Lützow. They were escorted into harbour by ten MTBs, on board which were most of the Senior Officers of the Nore Command flotillas. It was with mixed feelings that the British crews met face to face for the first time the enemy with whom they had fought so fiercely for five years. There was satisfaction, of course, for a battle well won. But also respect for an enemy who had shared common hardships in the bleak, storm-ridden narrow seas between Britain and the Continent of Europe.

EPILOGUE

Although Coastal Forces bore the brunt of the fighting against E-boats throughout the war, first with the short MGBs and MTBs and later mainly with the long 'D' type Fairmiles, the final defeat of this enemy threat was due largely to the close co-operation that was established between the Royal Navy and the Royal Air Force, particularly Coastal Command. As the operations described in this book have shown, it was not often that small fighting boats could sink one of their opposite numbers in the kind of fast-moving night engagements that were typical of coastal warfare. It was in combination with destroyers or fighter-bombers that the MTBs were most effective against their enemy.

The E-boats never had the advantage of such co-operation with their own naval and air services, partly due to a failure to appreciate fully the nature of coastal warfare and partly because of jealousies amongst the various services which continually plagued the German war effort. It was certainly not due to any lack of enterprise or daring on the part of the E-boat crews, in spite of an impression to the contrary which grew up in Coastal Forces. If for most of the war in the narrow seas the E-boats tended to avoid combat with MTBs, it was for the very good reason that there was little advantage to be gained from such actions. In view of the much greater use that Britain made of coastal shipping, the offensive was largely with the Germans and it was more important to sink a freighter loaded with coal, for instance, than an MTB. The E-boats themselves were generally the more effective craft; had they been given support by larger vessels together with air cover, they would certainly have been a much greater threat. Even as it was, they succeeded in tying down in home waters large defensive forces that were urgently needed elsewhere.

The E-boats fought more or less continually during the war in three theatres – the Western area (North Sea and English Channel), the Baltic and the Mediterranean, although it was in the former that they were most active. Of the 244 boats brought into operational service 146 were lost including 17 captured or requisitioned Allied craft; the 100 or so that remained after the war were divided among the victors in May 1945 and most of these later broken up for scrap. R-boat losses totalled 163 of the 326 brought into service. British Commonwealth warship losses due to direct attack by E-boats totalled some 40 ships of 25,000 tons, including two cruisers and seven destroyers. Allied merchant shipping sunk by E-boats in all waters totalled 99 ships of 229,676 tons. It is not possible to give a precise figure for the further number of ships sunk by mines laid by E-boats, as distinct from air or submarine minelaying, but it was likely to be around 20 per cent of the 534 merchant vessels (1,406,037 tons) lost by mines during the war. This would indicate that E-boats were responsible for about 2.5 per cent of the total 21,570,720 tons of Allied merchant shipping lost by all causes during the war, not a high proportion admittedly but the more significant because it was primarily coastal shipping.

The strength of Coastal Forces at the end of the war included 296 MTBs (with a further 80 in reserve), 26 MGBs (22 in reserve), 6 SGBs, and 940 MLs. Losses in action totalled 115 MTBs, 28 MGBs, 1 SGB and 79 MLs. German and Italian warship losses credited to Coastal Forces totalled 70 ships of 34,554 tons, including one cruiser, one armed merchant raider, five torpedo boats and one submarine; most of the remainder were German E-boats and R-boats. In addition, Coastal Forces sank 40 merchant ships of 59,650 tons in home waters, and (together with PT-boats) some 100 vessels of about 70,000 tons in the Mediterranean.

What emerges from these figures is that the E-boats were overall more successful against Allied merchant shipping than the MTBs against similar targets, but the MTBs achieved a greater degree of success against their opposite numbers. This is what one would expect, considering the larger amount of British coastal shipping available as targets to the Germans. And it was undoubtedly in laying mines that the E-boats achieved their greatest success. Some idea of the proportions can be gathered from the last five months of the war in home waters when, with few German aircraft in the air, nearly all the German mines were laid by E- and R-boats. Compared with six Allied ships totalling 12,972 tons sunk by torpedoes fired by E-boats, 25 ships totalling 75,999 tons were lost to mines. The craft of Coastal Forces, on the other hand, were used far less for the purpose of minelaying. In this respect, the greatest effect in disrupting German coastal traffic in home waters was achieved by air minelaying; during the RAF's campaign from April 1940 to the end of the war, no less than than 48,148 mines were laid by aircraft, resulting in the loss of 762 enemy merchant vessels and warships as well as 17 submarines (with damage to a further 196 ships and 17 E-boats), for the loss of 533 aircraft on minelaying sorties.

This was Bomber Command's biggest contribution to achieving victory at sea, but the value of air minelaying was little appreciated at the beginning of the war. In fact, neither side had given much consideration to the importance of coastal waters. It was a lesson that had to be re-learned from the past, with less excuse for Britain than for Germany in view of her greater naval tradition. Assessed against the overall war at sea, motor torpedo boats played a relatively minor role. But they were a highly significant factor in achieving and maintaining command of coastal waters, without which Germany found she could not invade the British Isles in 1940, and which also could have denied the Allies the ability to land in Normandy in 1944 had they not learned the lesson in time.

APPENDIX 1 ANTI·E·BOAT WEAPONS

The British suffered from a severe shortage of light weapons at the outbreak of World War II. This arose from the same cause as the shortage of high-speed engines – lack of pre-war research and investment.

Early MTBs were armed with .303in Lewis machine-guns, which fired too light a round to inflict serious damage on E-boats, even when grouped in quadruple mountings. To remedy this a twin Vickers .5in mounting was produced, but this gun was not very reliable and tended to jam. The US Navy also relied on a .5in machine-gun as the main armament of their PT boats for a long time, but the Browning was an altogether superior weapon. Fortunately for the British, the plans of the Oerlikon 20mm gun were obtained from Switzerland just before the fall of France in June 1940, and after lengthy delays in production the 20mm gun was issued to Coastal Forces. With its cyclic rate of 600 rounds per minute, one-man operation and drum-feed the Oerlikon was ideal for small craft. Towards the end of the war it also appeared as a twin hand-operated mounting, but tactical experience showed that a power-operated mounting was much more effective.

Destroyers, although much feared by E-boats because of their speed, manoeuvrability and gunpower, were at a disadvantage at close quarters because the 4in and 4.7in guns could not train fast enough. The first solution was to fit a hand-operated 2pdr (40mm) 'bow-chaser' right up in the bows of the ship, a position from which the gunner could rake an E-boat crossing the destroyer's bows. From this developed the idea of the twin 6pdr (57mm), which started life as an Army coast-defence weapon. After it had proved its worth against Italian MAS boats during an attack on Malta in July 1941, the Royal Navy took over a number of mountings and adapted them for shipboard use. The 6pdr Twin Mk1 normally fired 72 rounds per minute; the mounting weighed only 10cwt and required a crew of nine. To make it more lethal it was capable of 'blind fire' with the 271 and 272 radar sets. Although the effective range was only 5,000 yards the twin 6pdr had rapid training and 11° depression, and it proved deadly. Six destroyers were armed with the new gun in 'A' position in 1944.

The need for a bigger punch led to the development of power-operated versions of the single 2pdr, one an adaptation of the mounting used for the 20mm Oerlikon and the other developed by Rolls-Royce. These weapons were mounted in MGBs principally, and towards the end of the war a 6pdr version was produced. American PT boats bridged the gap by going to the Swedish 40mm Bofors gun, but this weapon was never available in sufficient numbers for the British to spare any for their Coastal Forces.

Although E-boats used mines and torpedoes, neither of these weapons was fully effective against them. Their high speed and shallow draught made them relatively immune to these forms of attack.

The E-boats' armament problems were nowhere near as difficult to solve as the British craft. From the outset the single 20mm gun was used, and the *S.38* series were armed with a 37mm gun based on the Swedish Bofors design. A twin 20mm mounting was added amidships in the later boats, and a Bofors 40mm superseded the 37mm anti-aircraft gun.

Towards the end of the war, when plans were made to double the torpedo-armament of the E-boat the gun-armament was also increased. The twin 20mm mounting was to be retained but a new single 30mm anti-aircraft gun was designed to be mounted forward and aft.

Other navies did not develop fast fighting craft to the pitch of the Allied and German navies, and so their boats never approached the others in scale of armament. There was a limit to the weight of guns which could be mounted in light craft. Vibration and the lively motion made fire-control difficult. The extra topweight and the limited number of positions in which guns could be mounted also imposed penalties on speed and seaworthiness which eventually became unacceptable.

APPENDIX 2
MINES

Two main types of mine were laid at sea by both the Axis and Allied powers during World War II – those which were moored and ground mines which rested on the seabed. Moored mines were either the contact variety, which fired when hit by a ship, or the influence type, detonated by some other means such as sound or a ship's magnetic field; ground mines were always the influence type.

Contact Mine. When dropped or lowered into the water, this type of mine was put into a ready-to-fire condition by a hydrostatic arming device which reacted at a predetermined water depth. There were basically two means of activating the firing mechanism when a ship struck the contact horn, either electrically by switching on the current from a battery, or chemically when the glass horn was broken; the Germans tended to favour the latter while the British preferred the former method. The earlier system of minesweeping required two ships steaming across a minefield and towing a wire rope between them with saw-like projections to cut the mooring lines; when the released mine floated to the surface it was harmlessly exploded by gunfire. Later developments included a system of paravanes and rudders to spread the tow-wires in a wedge shape from either side of a vessel, so that paths could be cleared by ships working individually.

Magnetic Mine. This principle was based on the fact that a steel ship acquires both permanent and induced magnetism, sufficient to explode a magnetic mine if passing sufficiently close. In order to prevent this, ships were equipped with 'degaussing' devices, basically coils of electrically charged wires placed around the hull to reverse the polarity of its magnetic field. Sweeping required the vessel concerned to produce a magnetic field strong enough to detonate such mines while far enough away not to cause damage. Eventually, a type of buoyant cable was developed through which an electric current could be pulsed; minesweepers towed two such lines on either side in a manner similar to sweeping contact mines.

Acoustic Mine. These mines were detonated by the sound of a ship's propellers or engines, picked up by a microphone and amplified. Because of accumulating silt or marine growth around the mine, an increasingly higher sound level was required to fire it. In addition, the continuous drain on the battery eventually sterilized such mines. Acoustic systems were most effective when combined with the magnetic type, the former being used to cock the firing mechanism and the latter then triggering the explosive. Sweeping was achieved by the use of mechanical noisemakers, such as an air-hammer beating on a steel plate; this could either be built-in or towed in a 'hammer-pot'.

Pressure Mine. This simple method made use of the principle that below a ship in motion in shallow water there is an area of reduced pressure, the extent depending on its speed and draught. Pressure mines contained a chamber divided in two by a diaphragm, one side open to the sea so that any change in pressure would bend it sufficiently to close a firing circuit and thus explode the mine. A small leak hole served to equalize the pressure on either side and prevent firing by slow changes in pressure such as those caused by tides. The outstanding advantage of this type of mine was that it was almost impossible to sweep. For that reason both sides were reluctant to use it and thus invite retaliation when neither had an effective counter-measure, although the Germans did employ it in 1944 and it was also developed in Britain. The best method of sweeping was to simulate the passage of a ship by towing a large expendable 'target' over the mine, but this was a slow procedure since the minesweeper had to reduce speed sufficiently not to explode it prematurely, and it was costly as well since the 'target' was often damaged. Heavy seas could sometimes activate such mines, and it was the gales off the Normandy beaches in particular that saved Allied minesweepers the necessity of clearing the defensive pressure mines laid by the Germans. The Americans developed an extremely effective pressure mine by combining it with either a magnetic or acoustic mechanism.

BIBLIOGRAPHY

Cobb, David, *Warship Profile No. 7* 'MTB/Vosper 70 ft': Profile Publications, 1972.

Cooper, Bryan, *The Battle of the Torpedo Boats*: Macdonald, 1970.

Dickens, Peter, *Night Action – MTB Flotilla at War*: Peter Davies, 1974.

Hichens, Robert, *We Fought Them in Gunboats*: Michael Joseph, 1944.

Hümmelchen, G, *Warship Profile No. 31* 'German Schnellboote': Profile Publications, 1973.

Roskill, S.W., *The War at Sea*: H.M.S.O.

Scott, Peter, *The Battle of the Narrow Seas*: Country Life, 1945.

INDEX

Ships' names and page references for illustrations are in bold type.

AA cannon, 20mm, **75**
AA gun, 37mm, 74, **74**
Anti-Aircraft Command, 81
Antwerp, **55**, 123
Armstrong, Captain H.T., 102
Arnold-Foster, Lt Mark, 103
Athenia, 32
Atlantic, Battle of, 34-5

Badger, 47
Baglietto shipyard, 27
Bailey, Lt G.E., 65
Baker, Lt G.H., 118
Barnet, Lt R.L., 97
Barrage balloons, **51, 117**
Bätge,Kapitänleutnant Niels, 61
Beehive, 47, 61
Bennett, Lt S.B.,83
Bergen, 40, **41**
Berthon, Lt P.A., 93
Bey, Kapitänleutnant Erich, 23
Borkum, 42-3
Boulogne, **55**, 85, 115, 116
BPB boats, 10, 25, 26, 27, 43, 45-6, 72, 73, 85
Bradford, Lt Donald Gould, 107, 117
Bristol engines, 73
Browning 0.5 Twin Machine Gun, **72**
Bulkeley, Lt-Cdr John, 115
Burk, Lt C.A., 111, 113
Bushnell, David, 13, 14
Bütow, Konteradmiral, 80

Calais, **55**, 85, 89
Campbell, Lt L.G.R., 65, 67, 88
Campbell, Sir Malcolm, 10
Camper and Nicholson craft, 73
Cane, Peter du, 25
Carl Peters, 40
Carr, Lt F.W., 102
Carr, Lt R.A., 88
Channel Force, 31
Channel Guard, 51
Channel Islands, The, **55**, 82, 88, 120
Chatham, **22** *see also Nore Command, The*
Cherbourg, **55**, 81, 86, 88, 106, 116, 117, 118
Clarkson, Lt V.F., 103
CMBs, 19, 25, 28
Coastal Forces (British), 9, 43, 57-9, 71, 73, 79-80, 86, 88, 91, 92, 101-102, 105, 109, 115, 118, 130-31; on the offensive, 93, 99; tactics, 93-4; new boats, 97; strength and disposition 1943, 108; strength at end of war, 127
Coastal shipping, 29-31, **54**, 57, 108, 114
Cobb, Lt H.P., 98
Convoys, 10, 30-35 passim, 38, 49-52, 55-6, 62, 81-2, 87-88, 92, 93, 97, 106, 114, 120, 123, 124, 127 *see also Coastal shipping*
Corburn, 42
Courageous 35

Daimler engines, 21-24 passim
Danielsen, Lt Per, 94

Danzig, Gulf of, 39
Dartmouth, 88, 98, 120
Davidson, Captain Hunter, 14
Davis, Lt-Cdr Richard 116,
'Degaussing girdle', 37
Den Helder, **22**, 123
Destroyers, 15-18, 32-3, 51-2, 82, 88, 94, 97, 106, 111-12, 126, 130-31
Detlefsen, Oberleutnant Hans, 45
Dickens, Lt-Cdr, 99-101, 103
Dieppe, **55**, 118
Dixon, Lt, 124
'Dog-boats', 72
Donnerwetter, 18
Dornier works, 78
Dover, **55**, 85
Dover Command, 85
Drayson, Sub Lt R.Q., 99
Dreyer, Christopher, 115
Duncan, Lt 'George', 88
Dunkirk, 45, **55**, 85

Eardley-Wilmot, Lt J.A., 48
E-boat Alley, 9, 83, 85, 106
E-boats, **6**, 8, 9, **16-17**, **23**, 39-42, passim, 61, **62**, **68**, **76**, **77**, 79, 105-6; origins, 10; descriptive diagram, **16-17**; first and second flotillas formed, 23-4; armaments, 23, 131; bases, 47-8, 52, 53, 82, 85, 86; mine laying, 53, 56, 61, 82, 83, 86, 88, 97, 121, 127; new types, 74-8; organisation, 80; tactics, 82, 88, 111, 112; first surrender to Coastal Forces, 84; attack on convoy, 86-7; successes, 92; threat diminishes, 92; losses, 107-8; role during invasion, 116-19; last major offensive, 123-4; final defeat, **120**, **122**, **123**, 124-5; summary, 126; and passim Individual boats and series: **S.1**, 21-23;· **S.2 – S.5**, 23; **S.6 – S.13**, 23; **S.14 – S.17**, 24; **S.18 – S.25**, 24; **S.26**, 39, 45; **S.30**, 40, 45, 63; **S.33**, 41-2; **S.41**, 63, 67-8, **68**; **S.80** series, **23**; **S.100** series, **23**, 87; **S.103**, 62-3; **S.208** series, 75-8; and passim
Edge, Lt P., 111
Elco (Electric Boat Company), 27, 28, 71, 79, 83
Ellis, Lt R.A., 58
Emdem,**22**, 108
Esmonde, Lt-Cdr E., 94
Ewerth, Oberleutnant, 22

Fairmile Marine Company Boats *see under* MGBs *and* MTBs
Faulkner, Lt R.I., 48
Feldt, Oberleutnant Klaus, 63, 86-7
Felixstowe, 43, 47, 61, 83, 88, 100
Fimmen, Oberleutnant Kurt, 45, 125
Fort William, 79-80
Foster, Lt, 124
Fowke, Lt M., 93
Friedrichshaven, 78
Fulton, Robert, 13-14

Gemmel, Lt-Cdr K., 102-3
Gniesenau, 94-5
Gotelee, Lt A., 98
Gould, Lt Stewart, 45, 85-6, 93-4
Great Yarmouth, **55**, 83, 106

Halifax Convoys, 34
Hall-Scott engines, 43, 46
Harris, Lt Allen, 116
Hart, Norman, 46
Havel I, 18
Heligoland, 39
Hichens, Robert Peverell, 64-70, 73, 85, 88, 99-100, 101
Higgins Industries boats, 27, 28, 71, 79, 115
Himmly, Professor, 14
Holmes, **95**
Hook of Holland, **55**, 82, 102, 113
Horne, Lt J.B.R., 83-4
Hornet, 15, 47
Howes, Lt Peter, 61
Humber, The, 32, 85
Humphreys, Lt J.F., 121
'Hunt' class Escort Destroyer, **52**

Ijmuiden. **55**, 82, 83, 111, 113, 115, 116, 121, 123
Isotta-Fraschini engines, 10, 26, 27, 43

Jaguar, 42
Jermain, Lt Dennis, 58
Johannsen, Kurt, 118

Karlsruhe, 40
Kekewich, Rear-Admiral Piers, 80, 101
Kelly, 42
Kemnade, Kptlt Friedrich, 47
Kiel, 24, **41**, 39, 47
Kirk, Admiral, 119
Kloche, Oberleutnant Joachim, 92

Klug, Kapitänleutnant, 63
Köln, 40
Komet, 99
Königsberg, 40
Kosky, Lt, 40-1
Kristiansand, 40, **41**
Künzel, Leutnant zur See, 62-3

Ladner, Lt T.R., 88
Law, Lt-Cdr Anthony, 117
Leaf, Lt Derek, 101, 112, 113
Lees, Captain D.M., 102
Le Havre, **55**, 116, 117, 118, 119
Le Touquet, 118
Lowestoft, **55**, 83
LS boats, 78
Luppis, Giovanni, 15
Lürssen boats, 8, 10, 19, 21, 23, 39-40, **62**, 68, 79
Lürssen Effekt, 8
Lürssen, Otto, 18
Lutzow, Kapitänleutnant,111, ·112

McIlwraith, Lt Alan, 90
McLaughlin, Captain P.V., 115
MAN engines, 22, 23, 24
Marshall, Lt R.M., 111-12
MAS boats, 8, 9, 20, 26-7, **27**, 63, 130
MA/SBs, 46-7, 51, 61, 72, 73
Maurice, Captain F.H.P., 101
May, Lt J., 124
Maybach engines, 21, 23
MGBs, 9, 11, **24**, **44**, 45-7, **46**, passim 73, **78**, **80**, 83, 85, 88, 111; Fairmile 'C', 46, 72, 89-91, 98, 107; first flotillas formed, 61; first successes against E-boats, 63-4, 66-70; long boats, 72; Fairmile 'D', 72, 94, 98, 102, 103, 111; armaments, 72, 131; bases, 85; successful action in channel, 88-91; cooperation with MTBs, 93 and passim; *see also Coastal Forces (British)*
Michel, 78
Mine Experimental Department, 37
Mines, 19, **34**, **35**, **36**, **37**, 38, 53-6, 85, 109-10, 121, 127-8; history, 13-15; laid in English Channel, 35; British minesweeping vessels, 55, 85; map showing British and German minefields, **34**; acoustic, 53-5, 109, 133 contact, **34**, **37**, 132; influence, **35**, 35

magnetic, 35-7, 53, 109, 132-3
pressure, 133
Minesweepers (British), 37
Mirbank Kapitänleutnant, 114, 116
MLs, 46, **46**, 51, 73, 83, 85, 109, 111, 115
Mobile Baloon Barage Flotilla, 51
Monson, Sir William, 13
Motor Torpedo Boats, 7-10, 14-20, 21-25, 28 see also E-boats and MTBs
MTBs, 8, 9, 11, 19, **25**, 26, **28**, 43-5, **52**, 73, 85, 102, 113-114, 124-5; first and second flotillas formed, 26; wartime role, 29-30, 58; at Zuidersee, 45; at Dunkirk, 45; bases, 47; tactics, 58-61, 100-101; long boats, 72; Fairmile 'D', 72, 94, 119, 121; armaments, 72, 130; cooperation with MGBs, 93; role during invasion, 115-121; *see also Coastal Forces (British)*
MTB/MGBs, 72-3, 103
Müller, Kapitänleutnant Karl, 106, 121

Napier engines, 26, 46
Newhaven, **55**, 104
Nordsee, 23
Nore Command, the, 30, 37, 55, 83, 86, 102, 103, 106, 111
North Sea, **41**

Oerlikon cannon, 20mm, **72**
Oheka II, 21
Opdenhoff, Oberleutnant, 42, 124
Operation 'Headache', 65, 66
Operation 'Weserübung', 39-40
Ostend, **55**, 82
Ouvry, Lt-Cdr J.G.D., 37

Packard engines, 10, 27, 28, 43, 45, 71, 72, 73
Perkins, Lt J.P., 101
Petersen, Kommodore Rudolph, 24, 40-1, 80, 116, 119
Plymouth, 30, **55**, 88, 92, 98, 106, 120
Plymouth Command, 86, 87
Portland, **22**, 31, 80
Portsmouth, 30, **55**, 88, 92, 97, 98, 106, 117, 119
Price, Lt G.D.A., 98
Prinz Eugen, 94-5
PT-boats, 8, 9, 10, 27-8, **27**, 71, 79, 94, 115-16, 117, 119-120, 130, 131
Pumphrey, Lt-Cdr, 93, 94

Raeder, Admiral, 31
RAF, Balloon Command, 81
   Bomber Command, 97, 127
   Coastal Command, 49, 97, 103, 108,
      109, 118, 126
   Fighter Command, 49, 81, 83, 103,
      108-9, 115
Ramsgate, 85, 89
R-boats, 8, 78, 82, 85, 88, 89-91, 97, 117,
   127
Richards, Lt G.D.K., 89-91, 103
Ritchie, Lt J.D., 97
Roeder, Oberleutnant Ullrich, 82
Rolls-Royce engines, 10, 26, 27
Roskill, Captain S.W., 82
Rosyth, 30, **69**, 106
Rosyth Escort Force, 33
Rotterdam, **55**, 108, 121, 123
Round, Lt M.V., 113

Sael, 40
Sapphire, 33
Saunders, Lt R., 103
Sayer, Lt-Cdr G.B., 26
S-boats *see E-boats*
Scapa Flow, 30, **69**, 32, 94
Scharnhorst, 94-5
Schlichting shipyard, 40
Schnellboote *see E-boats*
Scott, Lt-Cdr Peter, 97-8, 115
Scott-Paine, Hubert, 25, 26, 27, 28, 46
Searles, Lt Robert, 116
Seehund, 123-4
Segrave, Sir Henry, 10
Seine Bay, 118
SGBs 73, 85, 98, 104, 119; first flotilla
   formed, 97
Shaw, Lt D.A., 118
Short Sunderland Mk II, **109**
Sidebottom, Lt D.C., 89-90
Siemens, Wilhelm von, 18
Sobottka, Oberleutnant Walter, 106
Sonderkommando Gleitboot, 19
SO Torpedoboats, 40
Sparkman and Stephens, 27
Stayner, 95
Sterling engines, 71
Sturm, Kapitänleutnant Kurt, 24

Submarines, 'midget', 123-4 *see also U-boats*
SVAN shipbuilders, 18, 20, 26
Swinley, Cdr R.F.B., 102

TI boats, 28
Tamber, Lt-Cdr R.A., 102
Texel, **22**, 101
Thames Estuary defences, 81-2
Thompson, Sub-Lt P.A.R., 83-4
Thomson, Lt F.N., 121
Thornycroft boats, 10, 18, 19, 43, 71
Tirpitz, Admiral von, 14
Torpedoes, 19, 39, 59-60, **60-61**; history of,
   13-15; tubes, **62**, 63, 79; the 'Dackel',
   118; the 'Marder', 119; the 'Linsen', 119
Trelawny, Lt I.C., 103
Tsingtau, 23, 40
Tsurumi shipyard, 28

U-boats, 30, 31, 32, 35, 38, 42, 47, 49, 81

Valorous, 56
Vernon, 37
Vickers Twin .303 Machine gun, **65**
Vosper boats, 10, 26, 28, 43, 71, 73, 101,
   103

Ward, Lt B.C., 103
Wasp, 47
Watchman, 64
Weekes, Lt N.R., 90
Welman, Lt-Cdr A.E.P., 80
Weymouth, **55**, 102
White, J.S., 71
Whitehead, Robert, 15
Whitshed, 110
Wilhelmshaven, 24, 39, 40, **41**, 42, 63
Wilkie, Lt-Cdr D., 121
Worcester, Marquis of, 13
Wuppermann, Kptlt Siegfried, 40, 63

Yarrow, Alfred, 15
Yarrow shipyard, 15
Younghusband, Cdr J.L., 86

Zimmermann, Oberleutnant Wilhelm, 45
Zuiderzee, 45
Zymalkowski, Kapitan Felix, 86